WITNESS TO THE AMERICAN CENTURY

A LOOK BACK

"An Unexpected Life Well Led"

By
Marvin F. Moss

Dedication

To Father Kyrill (Stephen J. Juli), whose love made my life both better and richer, and to Father Mefodii, Abbot of the Skete of St. Maximos the Confessor and my patient spiritual guide. To my West Point classmates and to the 15 who gave their lives in Vietnam.

Acknowledgment

James Gelly and Richard Crampton, friends whose quizzing me about my service in Vietnam, led me ultimately to write this saga. Jack Brown, whose helpful suggestions assisted in framing it. Judy Mickelson, whose love and devotion have kept me sane. My brother, Philip and his family, whose quiet life of contemplation and learning is startlingly different from mine. My cousin Timothy Ingle and his family, whose unstinting love for Uncle Bud is a minor miracle. And finally, to my legions of friends who've enriched, challenged and emboldened my life.

About the Author

Marvin Moss entered West Point at the age of 17 launching a life dedicated to adventure, the pursuit of learning, love of public service, and his successful effort as a gay man to find someone to love. He fulfilled his lifelong motto "Qui vit sans folie n'est pas si sage qu'il croit" (he who lives without folly is not as wise as he believes) with over 80 years of lauded work as an Army officer, a senior aide on Capitol Hill, leader of various organizations at the national level and finally as one who transformed his retirement community in rural Virginia. An Orthodox Christian, he supported establishing the first Orthodox Monastery in Central Virgina. Recounted with humor and a profound understanding of the American people, he writes of a life of extraordinary achievements around the world, one he could only have dreamt of as he entered the gates of West Point 70 years ago.

Table of Contents

"The greatest genius is the most indebted man, someone deeply connected with others and who possesses a heart in unison with his time and country."

Ralph Waldo Emerson

"I am a person who never unlearned the enchantments of childhood," a quote by Michael Tilson Thomas

Introduction

After retiring from over 38 years of public service as a cadet, a soldier, a politician and later as a leader of a small rural community in Virginia and finally as a lay benefactor of an Eastern Orthodox monastery, I realized that this unlikely combination was strange enough to merit some elucidation. When I graduated from high school in Hagerstown, Maryland, in 1955 and entered the US Military Academy at West Point, I would never have imagined, or had the audacity to imagine, the direction my life would take or the experiences I would have, both in this country and abroad. Nor would I have been able to predict how American society and the world more broadly changed during my lifetime.

I entered elementary school in 1943 at the very beginning of an era of rapid change. A few years later, I remember vividly taking the public bus home from the movies with my grandfather and my brother and seeing the lights on late at night at the local high school filled with hundreds of World War II veterans studying under the GI Bill. The 1950's and 1960's were a period of unprecedented economic growth, a reduction in income inequality, and a huge increase in the middle class. Almost one-third of our workers belonged to unions. When I was born in 1937, my birth certificate listed my father's occupation as a "rough rounder." A rough rounder was a laborer in a shoe factory who removed excess leather from shoe soles. By 1946, after the war, my father was the prosperous owner of an independent insurance agency with 2 employees.

In 1937, Hagerstown, Maryland, was the second largest city in Maryland after Baltimore and the location of a number of major industries, including multiple shoe factories; the largest manufacturer of pipe organs in the world; Pangborn Corporation, one of the largest producers of sand blasting equipment; Fairchild Aircraft the producer of the Flying Boxcars for World War II and furniture factories. It was attractive to investors due to its location at the juncture of three major railroads, earning it the sobriquet "The Hub City." Of Maryland's smaller cities, it was the most industrialized. The city's makeup reflected the manufacturing economy of the time. The north end of town had wide boulevards with large houses culminating in North Potomac Street, which was lined with the impressive mansions of the owners and managers of its many factories. The east end was perhaps the poorest area with a small "little Italy" and a population living largely on the margins. Blue-collar workers were concentrated in the South and East Ends of town. Jonathan Street was the center of our large Black population. Schools were racially segregated, as were all public schools in Maryland at the time.

Hagerstown is now only a shadow of what it was in its glory days. Moller Pipe Organ, Fairchild Aircraft and Pangborn all closed years ago. The city's unemployment rate is almost always higher than the state average. Hagerstown, in addition to being a rail hub, became an interstate hub, with two major interstates passing near the city potentially an advantage but, in reality, serving as an incentive to empty out its downtown businesses. In some ways, the decline of Hagerstown could serve as a metaphor for what was happening throughout vast sections of industrial America, especially in the Midwest. Think Akron, Toledo and South Bend.

Even at an early age, I was experiencing rapid change around me, although I may not have recognized it as such at the time. But some elements of those changes led me to believe I could ferret out their perilous implications. At the end of my plebe year at West Point, my father, Benjamin F. Moss, was president of the local Kiwanis Club and invited me to speak to the group at its monthly lunch. He asked me to talk about West Point and my experience there. I, without consulting him, decided to broaden my talk to other issues.

At that time, the Washington County school system was arguably one of the best in the country. Its superintendent, for instance, was hired away based on that success to head up the Chicago public schools. One result was that the Ford Foundation then gave a large grant to our schools to install a very extensive closed-circuit television system linking all the classrooms to a central studio. I realized the implications immediately and said in my talk that I thought it was a mistake and could, in the long run, have a seriously detrimental effect on the quality of instruction. When I got in the car with Dad, he was furious. It seems he had just gotten the contract to insure the entire Ford network. The advent of television also fascinated me. We had one of the first tv sets in town which drew my friends to our house in a steady stream, and as I observed them, I saw the powerful pull of this new gadget and felt that it had the potential for being at the same time a benefit to society, a threat to family cohesion and a distraction from many important things including reading and social interaction.

My life, almost from its outset, was, to put it mildly, a bit odd and unpredictable. I have always viewed myself, even from a young age, as "different." I suppose the most succinct way of expressing this is to say that I succeeded in life in ways that, to this day, continue to surprise and startle me. In doing so, I became a witness not only to the vicissitudes of life around the world but also to those in American society. Therefore, this life story encompasses a period of profound reorientation in the United States and elsewhere. I am not a sociologist or a political demographer, nor do I pretend to be an expert in the more arcane aspects of political science. However, I do count myself as a keen observer of the worlds I've inhabited for over 86 years.

After retiring in 1995 from my job as chief of staff to US Senator Paul S. Sarbanes (D-MD) for 18 years, I gave a lecture at Salisbury State University on Maryland's Eastern Shore and at Ball State University in Muncie, Indiana, entitled "American Democracy at the End of the American Century." Preparing for that lecture forced me to focus on our country through a wide-angle lens, to think seriously about how our society had changed throughout my lifetime and to attempt an analysis of where those many changes could lead us. At the end of that lecture, I concluded that America's cohesiveness, trust in government and other institutions, and sense of common purpose had eroded to the point that democracy itself could, at some future date, be in peril. Despite that relatively gloomy conclusion, I did not presage this nation's becoming the tribal red and blue camps that now exist, which are clearly inimical to its future.

At a very early age, I became aware that I was homosexual. Despite my somewhat feeble efforts along the way to convince myself otherwise, I finally and rather joyfully accepted that that was who I was. I had to accommodate myself to that reality. I then made another decision, which has guided my life ever since. I refused to let my being gay interfere with my life and my work as an adult. I also realized that finding someone to love would become a challenge. My life, as described in perhaps too much detail in this rambling saga, clearly indicates that I succeeded both in finding someone to love and in having my career blossom.

I would be remiss if I did not write about the trauma of hiding my homosexuality for the first thirty years or so of my adult life. I believe that being a naturally gregarious, voluble and outgoing man made this problem less dramatic. That said, it was still a formidable challenge, so I was constantly on guard and living in fear, especially in the Army, that my secret would be exposed. I recall my concern vividly as I was investigated many times in order to get higher and higher security clearances. Either my friends, who knew I was gay and were interviewed, lied, or the investigators simply asked the wrong questions.

It would be difficult to exaggerate the anxiety associated with being gay when I was in my youth. A recent book, "Secret City: The Hidden History of Gay Washington," by James Kirchik, does a masterful job of detailing this somewhat sordid history. In the late 1950's and into the 1960's, there was what he calls a

"Lavender Menace" inextricably linked to the Red Scare. He writes that at the height of the Cold War, "It was safer to be a Communist than it was to be a homosexual."

And now! At my 55th West Point reunion in 2014, the armed services had just recently ended its ridiculous "Don't Ask, Don't Tell" policy, so I asked the authorities if I could meet with two openly gay cadets, a man and a woman. I can only guess their initial reaction. I was asked to send a CV and to prove that I was not a serial killer, pervert or deviant from outer space. I evidently convinced them that I was an upstanding, relatively normal citizen. I met with two charming, forthcoming cadets at their social hall, had a conversation which included my relating to them my history of being a closeted gay, and gleaned from them that their being openly gay was not a problem. There is now a gay club at West Point called "Knights Out."

The three of us also discussed the anomaly that some of the greatest warriors in history were undoubtedly gay, including Alexander the Great, King Frederick the Great of Prussia and Lord Kitchener. An entire unit of the army of ancient Thebes was made up of male lovers. I'd also long ago concluded, based on no evidence whatsoever, that Douglas MacArthur was probably one of the greatest closet cases. Wow! Did that one blow your mind? I posit that the treatment of gay characters in film, but especially on tv has had a great impact on the acceptance of gay people and the enormous changes in the law normalizing and accepting gay relationships. I, of course, celebrate that, but recognize that with the Supreme Court having now become what I call the "Bork" court, much of this progress could be undone.

This memoir will not only give a detailed history of my life but also show how I was changing with the times and how those changes were affecting my development and career.

Who exactly is Marvin? I have surprised myself by living for a most unexpectedly adventurous and episodic 80+ years during which I fell in love, garnered an untold number of friends, defended my nation in a war which I opposed, served my country on congressional staff, became a celibate brother in an Orthodox monastery and survived to regale one and all with outlandish but invariably true tales of my escapades around the globe. When introduced at a public meeting in 2009, my host, after reviewing my resume, said, "You made this up, of course." I did not make it up. So here we begin. Marvin is Marvin F. Moss.

Chapter 1
The Beginning

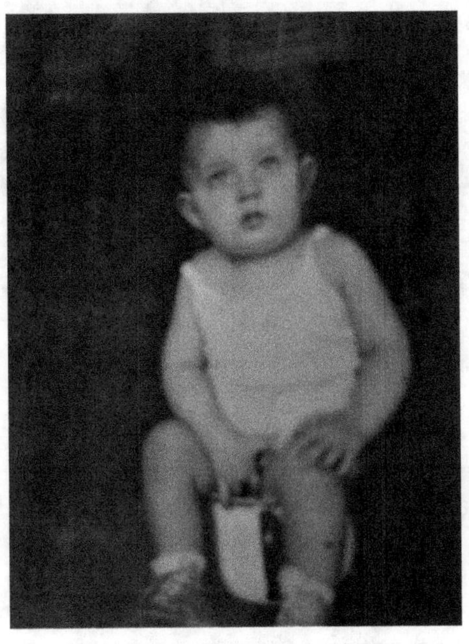

Born on October 4, 1937, I was evidently obstreperous, difficult, histrionic, charming and remarkably inarticulate. Mom reported that, in order to get attention, I would constantly lie on my back on the kitchen floor, stomp my feet and bellow loudly. After many repetitions of this, my family simply ignored me. I was very late both in learning to walk and in getting the hang of potty training, as the above photo attests (mom's caption for it is simply "trying"). I evidently never said "Mama" or "Daddy" as most children do as their first words. But since mom was reading the wonderful book, "Ferdinand the Bull" to me regularly, my first utterance was, "Ferdinand, out of the barn."

It appears that gender confusion was part of my early upbringing, as this photo suggests. Mom sent it to a photographer to tint, and he, thinking I was a cute little girl (the chubby one on the far left), put a pink ribbon in my hair. Come to think of it, I do look like a girl.

**Our Uncle West Point Cadet
Marvin Jacobs with Phil and Me, 1938**

I had a Charlie McCarthy doll at age 4 that I carried everywhere I went. Mom would give me a small box of raisins to eat as a snack, but I fed all of them to Charlie once I discovered he was empty inside. We raised pigeons, which Grandfather PapPap Jacobs trapped for us. He built a coop for us under the back porch. They bred like rabbits, and there were soon zillions of them. Mom rebelled and ordered us to let them go. We opened the cage, they all flew away, and in the evening, they were back exactly where they'd come from. Mom promptly had the cage dismantled.

We built a clubhouse in a wooded area across from the Western Maryland Railroad tracks. For our gang, it was a secret haunt, and we hung out there almost every day, hiding from our parents and the outside world. One day, I had the bright idea of having all of us, boys and girls, disrobe and do a festive sort of Indian dance. It was great innocent fun. The next day, when I arrived home from school, Mom was waiting for me with a scowl on her face. One of the kids had squealed to his parents. She quizzed me about my goading my confreres to dance naked in the woods. I, of course, admitted it. She told me that I was never to do that again without explaining why.

During the early days of World War II, my father and grandfather were recruited as area Air Raid Wardens, which meant that when the sirens went off, they donned sashes and white helmets and went out to ensure that every house in the neighborhood had its lights out. This was great fun for us since it meant that members of our family were important for just a brief moment. Even then, I wondered why or how the Germans would bomb our neighborhood, which was 150 miles from the sea.

My penchant for profligacy evidenced itself at an early age. We lived two blocks from the county fairgrounds and a half-mile race track. My gang would buy a big block of ice from the neighboring ice house and, with many different flavors prepared by our mothers, head off to the races to make snowballs and to earn some money. I was never permitted to participate since I'd already spent my allowance on other things, so I was unable to contribute to buying the block of ice. I would tag along behind them, sadly feeling left out.

Our father was known as a bit of a character, as was Pappy Ebersole, who lived in the apartment in our house. Pappy was the manager of the Newberry five-and-dime store in town. One Christmas, we were awaiting my father so we could go to midnight services at our church, where I sang angelically in the junior choir. He arrived very late and quite drunk. It seems he'd bought Phil and me each a new bicycle for Christmas. After his office party, he and Pappy were riding the bikes up the main street in Hagerstown when they were arrested for drunken bicycle riding. We were delighted both with the story and our present.

It was a big deal when the movie "Gone with the Wind" came to Hagerstown's largest and most ornate movie palace, the Maryland Theater. Pappap took Phil and me to see the movie, and all went well until the little girl in the movie was jumping over an obstacle with her pony, fell off and died. I immediately became utterly hysterical. Poor Pappap gave up trying to silence his little screaming grandson and fled the theater. The poor man never did get to see the rest of the movie.

On May 8, 1945, Germany surrendered to the Allied forces, which set off a massive national celebration. I was visiting my friends who worked at the T.S. Michael ice plant near our house when Pappap came to get me. He led Phil and me down North Potomac Street, filled with cars honking their horns in celebration. By the time we got to the city square, it was already filled with thousands of people hugging each other, kissing and otherwise expressing their great joy. It was a memorable day; one I shall never forget.

In 1949, our maternal grandfather, Roy B. Jacobs, died after a hernia operation. We were devastated since he was both a role model and a great friend to us, having lived with us since we were born.

Our Much-Loved Pappap, Roy B. Jacobs

Chapter 2

My Epiphany

During the summer of 1951, my family was visited by my uncle, Marvin Jacobs, and his family. He was our mother's only sibling and a graduate of West Point with the class of 1940, where he excelled in academics and stood at the top of his class. At that time, he was chief of staff to the Governor of the Panama Canal Zone, a position effectively making him the second in command. In the course of their visit, he suggested to my parents that my brother, Philip, and I should go to Panama that summer for a visit. To our great delight and obvious surprise, our parents agreed, bolstering my already nascent fascination with travel and adventure. Thus began my epiphany.

Mother took us by car to stay with cousins in a town near Harrisburg, Pennsylvania, in preparation for putting us on the train to New York and, hence, by boat to Panama. Phil was 14, and I was 13. It is difficult to imagine today sending two young teenagers to the big city on the train without an escort, but there we were, and we were ecstatic. I had done some research in preparation for the trip, including sights we might encounter along the way. One such was Pennsylvania Station, one of the most imposing and magnificent Beaux-Art buildings in the country. At the time it opened in 1910, it was the world's largest and most modern train station. Needless to say, I was not disappointed once our train pulled into the station, and we hauled our bags through the concourse to the taxi stand. Here is what we saw:

That moment is forever etched in my memory. Even at that early age, the building epitomized my view of what human beings were capable of doing to enhance the joy of travel. Years later, I was devastated when it was razed and replaced by a modern, intensely ugly and dysfunctional new terminal. As the invincible Vincent Scully once opined about the contrast between the two: "Then one entered the city like a god. One scuttles in now like a rat." This was perhaps the beginning of my lifelong interest in and fascination with architecture and history.

We caught a taxi to Pier 64, where our ship, the <u>SS Panama</u>, was berthed. The <u>Panama</u> and her sister ships, the <u>Ancon</u> and the <u>Cristobal,</u> were built for the Panama Canal Company in 1939, and at the time of their launching were perhaps the most modern and safest vessels afloat. In addition, the interior design of all three identical ships had been done by Raymond Loewy, one of America's premier industrial designers. All suites on board were first class with spacious bedrooms/sitting rooms and a view of the sea. All three ran a regular schedule of voyages from New York to Colon in the Canal Zone, normally a trip of 7 or 8 days.

The SS Ancon, sister to the Panama

Phil and I were to meet our Aunt Mary Jacobs (Uncle Marvin's wife) and her two children, Anne and Roy, at the ship in order for Aunt Mary to ensure that our high jinks were both monitored and curtailed. Mother had packed cheese sandwiches for us to eat on the train. When we arrived at the pier about two hours before boarding, Phil, perhaps overcome by the sandwiches and excitement, suddenly became nauseous. I was a bit terrified and unsure about what to do; however, I steeled up my courage and entered the pier. I found a purser who very kindly came and took Phil and our luggage on board the ship. I was then sitting alone, rather forlornly, at the pier's entrance. Then it dawned on me that my mother had pinned our Panama entrance documents in our luggage, which had now been taken on board with Phil. Meanwhile, no Aunt Mary.

Thus began the first real test of my sagacity and blooming maturity. When boarding finally began, I explained to the customs official that my official papers were already on board with Phil. He then took me on the ship, searched out our stateroom, found our papers and left me very happily on board. I was relieved to see that Phil had recovered and was resting comfortably. Still no Aunt Mary.

About 20 minutes before the Panama was scheduled to sail, we had to make a decision. So, Phil and I put our heads together, and I suggested that it was important that we sail even if Aunt Mary and the kids did not appear. He agreed while recognizing that it was both daring and perhaps foolhardy. With just minutes left, the Jacobs arrived. We all went on the top deck to watch our departure cruising down the Hudson past the towers of lower Manhattan, the inner harbor, Governor's Island and the Statue of Liberty.

The voyage was both memorable and uneventful for the first 4 days or so. We were surprised to be living in such luxury, to be treated as young adults, and for the first time ever, being able to choose what we wanted to eat in the attractive Art Deco dining room. That all changed when we entered the Caribbean and skirted a severe tropical storm. For some unknown reason, I was the only one in the family not to be seasick. I, therefore, took on the responsibility of looking after Phil and the three Jacobs, who were also seriously indisposed. I was feeding Phil soda crackers, his only sustenance for several days, since he was unable to make it to the dining room. As we approached Colon, calm seas once again prevailed.

Uncle Marvin met us in Colon. Mom and Dad had given us a fairly handsome amount of money to buy each of us a Swiss watch, figurines, and an assortment of other things. Aunt Mary helped guide us through this rather reckless extravaganza. I bought a simple but elegant Movado watch. Other than the watches, the rest was shipped home. In port at that time was the majestic battleship Missouri, on which the documents had been signed by the US and Japan ending the war in 1945. Uncle Marvin arranged for us to visit the ship and see the plaque marking the site of the ceremony. We then drove across the Isthmus to the Jacobs' quarters in Pacific Heights.

The second evening, we managed to embarrass our poor Aunt Mary, who was a stickler for protocol and very rank conscious. They invited General and Mrs. Francis K. Newcomer to dinner and to play bridge. Aunt Mary, perhaps unaware that Phil and I had been playing bridge together since I was 6 and he, 7, seated us as the opponents of the Governor of the Canal Zone and his wife, assuming we were easy prey. General Newcomer was a West Point graduate who graduated at the top of his class. Although we were not great players, we were used to playing together and knew our bidding system by heart. It shocked them and Aunt Mary that they never won a single rubber. We were privately quite pleased with ourselves.

There were two highlights of the trip. The first was to see the transiting of the Aircraft carrier, the USS Wasp, through the Miraflores Locks. We were in the control tower when the electric "mules" pulled the giant carrier into the locks with only inches to spare on each side. The flight deck was so high that the awnings on the control tower had to be lowered to allow it to pass. We were, in reality, looking up at the flight deck as it headed west toward the Pacific.

The second was a memorable trip Uncle Marvin took us on to retrieve data from the rain gauges on the Chagres River, which flows into Gatun Lake and is the principal source of water vital to the functioning of the canal. We crossed the lake by motor launch and then boarded wooden dugout canoes, which took us upriver. At several rapids, the Panamanian crews had to portage the canoes. The jungle was amazing. Among other exciting sights were the iridescent giant blue butterflies flitting around.

When we arrived at our destination, Phil and I skinny dipped in the clear water of the Chagres while keeping a wary eye out for the venomous snake, the fer de lance.

We visited Panama City, which then consisted mostly of small retail stores, tiny houses clustered around plazas and an air of southern indolence. How times have changed! Panama now owns and operates the canal to the tune of $3.3 billion in annual revenue and has become a retirement haven for retirees, including many from the US. It now has a skyline similar to Miami's.

At the end of the summer, we flew home via Miami to be met at National Airport by our anxious parents. I could not wait to answer my classmates' question when school started again: "What did you do this summer?" Thus, my parents inadvertently launched Marvin into the unknowing world. I believe this trip had a profound effect on my approach to life and triggered a lifelong passion for travel and new adventures.

Chapter 3

Vignettes from my Youth

Phil and I, while living in Hagerstown on Fairground Avenue, attended elementary school at two nearby public schools, Wayside and Broadway. The students mostly came from the most prosperous part of town, the North End, although our Fairground Avenue was still home to many lower-middle-income families. Our house was bought by our maternal grandfather. He lived there as well as our parents, and in an apartment on the top floor, the Ebersole family of three. It was a tad crowded.

It was an easy walk to school from our house, and as we strolled along, we gathered with other friends headed in the same direction. I can't remember when this happened, but Dad bought a Packard limousine with a 12-cylinder engine, a glass divider between the chauffeur and the passengers, cigar lighters in the back, and a sound system allowing one to speak to the driver. Dad hired a local drunk to drive us to school despite our being within easy walking distance. We would pick up our friends and merrily head off. We became very popular until mom revolted and forced dad to fire the driver and get rid of our beloved conveyance.

I attended classes there through the fifth grade when we moved to our farm south of the city and began attending Howard Street School. I immediately noticed that the students were slightly different in that they generally came from families with fathers working in factories. Then on to junior high at South Potomac Junior High School, where in the 9th grade, I was elected captain of the safety patrol, an important position in those days.

I was even in those days known for being less than a stellar athlete. But there were two incidents that proved otherwise. In the 9th grade, in our English classroom, the city had installed a huge voting machine that clearly stated on the side that it weighed over 800 pounds. My jock friends were trying to lift it an inch or so from the floor. I was watching them and discovered their mistake. They were attempting to lift it by bending over and using their backs. They were laughing at me when I went back to try. I stooped down, and using my strong legs, I lifted it several inches off the floor and then dropped it with a great bang. They were astounded. I never told them that I had won using brain over brawn. Several weeks later, we had a field day with competitive sports. I won both the 100-yard dash and the hop, step and jump to the amazement of all. I won the latter event by thinking of myself as a bird when I took off for the jump portion. I won by a sizeable margin thanks to my imagination.

Hagerstown High School was remarkable for its generally great teachers, many of whom were spinsters. I was in the academic stream and had Rachel Sheets as my English teacher and Enid Long for math. Miss Sheets undoubtedly had the greatest influence on my life of any teacher. She was a disciplinarian with high expectations. She gave us 15 new vocabulary words each week on Friday and tested us on them the next Tuesday, asking for both the definition and the word's use in a sentence. She was also a Shakespeare nut, as was I. I had a book of the plays with snippets from each, memorized one quote each week and challenged her to identify the play. She usually succeeded. She liked the game. Despite her somewhat dramatic air, she was usually calm and debonair. However, once each year, she descended into sheer madness by acting out Lady Macbeth's sleepwalking or mad scene. It was amazing to watch her transformation into a raging monster before our eyes. She'd pushed her desk up against the blackboard before the performance began. She wound up leaping onto her desk and madly clawing the blackboard with her long, shiny fingernails while declaiming, "Out, out damn spot." It was mesmerizing.

We also had our fair share of crackpot teachers. First among them was Homer Kaylor, who taught (well, sort of taught) Problems of Democracy. He was also a bit frightening to look at, with long hair sprouting from his nose. His claim to fame was our annual trip to the nearby Antietam battlefield, where, along Bloody Lane, the most gruesome part of any American battlefield, he would declaim a long poem about the battle. Other than that, we learned nothing in his class. I eventually wrote a poem about him. It went: "Mister Kaylor, porcupine nose, don't you worry, don't you fret. The Little men in white will get you yet."

I edited the yearbook and wrote for the school's newspaper. I was elected the friendliest boy by my class. I had a crush on several of my classmates, feelings I had to hide. I hosted many parties at our farm and was both gregarious and charming. Our father continued his unblemished record of being a hapless farmer, having just received a goat from a client in arrears. Phil and I named him Ben after our father. With the goat came its little goat cart. The goat immediately killed all the fruit trees in our orchard by eating the bark. At one of my parties, I hooked Ben to his cart and put a friend, Anita Lesher, in it, not knowing what was going to happen. Ben leaped over the boxwood hedge, leaving Anita sprawled on the ground.

My childhood years in retrospect seem idyllic. The country was making significant strides in multiple directions. An increasing number of women were seeking employment, largely based on the work they did in various capacities, including in factories during the war. In 1947, President Truman integrated the armed forces. Prior to World War II, few families paid income taxes, which were targeted at the wealthy. After the war, families, including mine, began paying income taxes and accepted it as a given to support the fiscal needs of a global conflict. More people could now afford to buy a house or rent a decent apartment. The concept of suburban life emerged with the development of Levittown and other communities on the fringes of major cities. The GI Bill produced thousands of newly educated and trained men who helped drive the rapid economic growth.

My own family was thriving. We were able to transition from a breadwinner who was a laborer to a man who owned his own successful business. We moved from a crowded house in town shared with another family to a large, imposing farmhouse on 18 idyllic acres in the countryside. Phil and I had benefited from a first-rate public education system. We had been exposed to international travel and to a bevy of interesting and peculiar characters. We, in fact, felt very secure and positive about our futures and about that of our nation. Naïve perhaps, but then we were young. Naivete is perhaps one of the blessings of youth.

I will never forget the reaction when I first brought some of my friends from South Potomac Junior High School to our farmhouse for a visit. I'd taken for granted that a large, substantial brick house with over 4,500 square feet was typical. My classmates very quickly let me know that I lived in a fantasy world. They were in awe of our house and considered me and my family to be wealthy and quite different from theirs. This was a revelation to me a rather stark reminder that my way of life was considerably different from that of most of my classmates, who came from the South End of Hagerstown and were children of middle-income working families.

Our father frequently hung out at the Vogue Room in Hagerstown, his favorite haunt after work leading to a number of strange occasions. He invited one of the musicians, a jazz pianist who was appearing there, to come home, stay for several days and teach me a completely new and improvisational way of playing the piano. I hated it. Next came a couple who were also performers at the Vogue Room, specializing in the American Songbook. They camped out with us for several weeks, entertaining us in the evening with Gershwin and Porter. Mother finally realized they were mooching off us and threw them out.

Last but not least of my father's acquisitions was our beloved Mr. Frank Zaccaria, who was brought home by dad to be our "tenant farmer" on our stupendous 18-acre spread. He was utterly delightful. He looked and smelled of Italy. He smoked cigars and then made guitars out of their boxes. He would sit outside his home, the summer kitchen in back of the main house, strum his guitar and sing 'Ah Maria' endlessly. He scoured the fields for greens to make into his beloved salads. He was always smiling. Once, he asked me to take him to the bus station in Hagerstown so he could visit relatives in New Jersey. He wrapped his homemade sausages in brown paper, which was then covered with grease, and carried bundles of other goodies. I watched, and when he got on the bus, everyone moved away from him. In my second year at West Point, I was in the field at Camp Buckner for summer training when an MP came looking for me to tell me that there was a strange man at the gate looking to visit me. Sure enough, it was our dear Mr. Frank. I could immediately tell that he was ailing, and then he said to me. "Mr. Marby (he could never pronounce Marvin), I no can piss." It seems he was having an attack of prostatitis. I was delighted to see him, but I also needed to help him. I arranged for the MPs to take him to a doctor in Highland Falls to treat him for his condition. Years later, after dad died, he returned to Hagerstown for a visit, and with a twinkle in his eyes, he said to mom, "Miss Louisa, you rich woman. I marry you and take you away to Italy." Mom was delighted but politely declined.

It is, however, easy to forget the more alarming aspects of this period. The drills in high school involved diving under your desk in case of a nuclear attack. The constant drumbeat of public declarations regarding the Red Scare both domestically and internationally. Elections in Italy brought the Communists into a coalition government. The Berlin Airlift. The fall of the Chinese

Nationalists. The Soviet atomic bombs. The advent of McCarthyism. The Amy McCarthy hearings. The firing of General MacArthur. The Korean War*. The list could go on and on.

*A funny comment about that. The day the war broke out, I came home from school. Our mother was getting in the car to leave. I asked her where she was going, and she replied: "I'm going to town to get all the food before the hoarders get it." Even then, I found that very funny.

How then do I consider my life to have been idyllic? I suppose, despite the gravity of many of these conundrums, life on a farm outside Hagerstown, MD, seemed to be largely removed from the reality of these events. Even with the advent of television and the broadcasting of much of this news, it still appeared to us as an abstraction. My family was prosperous. Hagerstown was booming. I was living in a world of endless possibilities, at least from my probably naïve perspective, despite realizing the potential gravity of these rather ominous developments.

Chapter 4

A Gay Boy Goes to West Point

When I was a junior in high school, my older brother and I had been trundled off to Hagerstown Business College in the summer. HBC was, in those days, a rather startling anachronism, since it was the same school our mother had attended 30 years earlier to learn stenography, and it looked like that. It was musty, dark, and unwelcoming, headed by the single Funk siblings, brother and sister, who were not only dour but downright frightening. We sat at individual typewriters and, once taught the fingering system, were required to type with the keyboards covered. I found all of this slightly hysterical, but I excelled nonetheless. This newly acquired typing skill would later cause problems for me during my Plebe year at West Point.

Six weeks after graduating near the top of my class at Hagerstown High School, I entered the United States Military Academy at West Point as a cadet having received an appointment from my Congressman, Dewitt Hyde, representing Maryland's Sixth District. I aced the SOLs and later the much more difficult West Point entrance exams, which were administered en masse at the Forest Glen Annex of the Walter Reed Army Hospital. We were also subjected to a thorough physical/medical examination during which it was discovered that I had scoliosis or lateral curvature of the spine, which meant my body tilted slightly to the right by about 15 degrees, a condition that caused me great anxiety later at the academy. I presumed this condition was caused by the fact that I evidently was very late in learning to walk, but could scoot along the floor in a crawl at a remarkable speed. Reading my medical report, I also gleaned that the Terry Thomas-like gap between my front teeth, which I rather liked, was called a 4-millimeter diosmas. A psychologist interviewed each one of us individually. When asked if I had any phobias, I opined that I was afraid of butterflies, a revelation the examiner obviously did not take seriously. However, it was true then and is still true to this day. Later, in 1968, on my way to Vietnam, I was praying that there would be no butterflies.

My interest in qualifying for West Point stemmed mainly from my Uncle Marvin Jacobs. When I was 4 or 5, mom made both of us little West Point uniforms, which were wool and itched uncomfortably. Perhaps I was fated to go to West Point, as this photograph attests.

I'd also applied to Dartmouth College and Harvard University. To my amazement, in March 1955, I was accepted at all three and had to make a choice. For a variety of reasons, none of which was logical or anticipated, I chose to go to the academy. That decision shocked many of my friends and my parents, although my father, Benjamin F. Moss, a successful businessman, was relieved not to have to pay the steep tuition at the civilian schools. My mother, Louise Moss, reluctantly accepted that I was about to enter an environment for which I was uniquely unsuited. I also suspected that she had already surmised I was a budding homosexual.

As soon as I was accepted at West Point, I realized that I had to do something about my rather miserable physical condition. The material I received from the academy suggested that I buy a pair of plain black shoes to break them in before matriculating. I did so. So, from March on, I walked almost 9 miles each evening in my spiffy new shoes from Hagerstown High School, which was in the far north of town, to my home in the country some five miles south of town. From the south end, I walked on the railroad tracks, which ran behind our small farm. While doing so, I had lots of time to think about what was happening to me, including some fantasies about my future. I was surprised that my parents still assumed that, once I graduated from West Point and fulfilled my service obligation, I would return to my hometown and join Dad's insurance business. My brother, Phil, was at Rose Poly at the time, and I had the distinct impression that he, too, had no desire to be an insurance salesman. I did not disabuse them of their notion; however, I felt guilty that my silence might have misled them.

I was attracted to men as soon as I discovered the joy of sex at the age of 13 while staring at a photo of Charles Adams in my bedroom closet, an appropriate location for such activity. My closet was where I stored all my treasures, including maps, travel brochures, my stamp collection, and every article about the new US superliner, the _SS United States_. The collection hinted at a barely repressed desire for wanderlust as well as just plain lust. I was very popular in high school, having been voted the friendliest boy and editor of the class yearbook. I dated one of the female cheerleaders, Janie Newkirk, who became my steady but platonic friend. I was dreadful at athletics and very slow to evince any of the manifestations of puberty so rampant with my contemporaries. This also led to some trying moments in my first year at West Point.

I knew a great deal about West Point, its traditions, its first year of relentless hazing, and its requirement to memorize a whole series of nonsense sayings; thus, I was better prepared than many, having already learned most of the Plebe "poop," as it was so indelicately called. I especially liked them, and to this day still know the Definition of Leather (why this particular piece of doggerel was thrust upon us is itself a mystery). It goes: "Sir, the definition of leather. If the fresh skin of an animal, cleaned and divested of hair, fat and other extraneous matter, is immersed in a dilute solution of tannic acid, a chemical combination ensues. The gelatinous tissue of the skin is converted into a non-putrescible substance impervious to and insoluble in water. This,

Sir, is leather." To this day, it is difficult for me to imagine that my wallet, shoes and belt are non-putrescible substances.

In 1955, West Point was intent on teaching incoming cadets the importance of military courtesy and decorum, including how to leave one's calling card unobtrusively when first meeting one's commanding officer and his wife. My favorite part was our dancing lessons. You must remember that there were no women cadets in those dark, woebegone days, so we had to dance with each other. The instructor they hired was from the Arthur Murray Studio, a woman with a very loud Brooklyn accent who kept yelling at us, "Stop marching." I loved it. Then, to highlight the absurdity of it all, she put on a record of Frank Sinatra singing "I'm in the mood for love." While being held tightly by one of my handsome classmates, I was chuckling at the incongruity of it all. I honestly believe I was the only one who delighted in the irony of a roomful of young men all dancing with each other.

The first summer at the academy is called Beast Barracks, and it certainly deserves such a name. My first roommate was a charismatic, very fit Native American named Charlie Rainwater. He could run circles around me. To my amazement, after several weeks, he simply disappeared and headed home to Georgia. As the assistant football coach in Hagerstown had said to me, "Marvin, you will have no problem with academics, but you will have a tough time with the physical aspects." Oh, so true. One of my first trials was bayonet drill on the Plain, the West Point parade field. We were asked to hoist our rifles with their fixed bayonets and charge a dummy with ferocious, blood-curdling screams. My efforts were time and again deemed to be insufficiently violent, so I had to repeat them an untold number of times in 90-degree heat. I almost passed out, but hung in there. Needless to say, I lost 15 pounds in the first month and, by the end of August, weighed only 128 pounds. Years later, at one of our reunions, my classmate, John Wilson, who was in my Beast Barracks platoon, said to me, "Marvin, in my motivational talks, I always use you as an example of courage." I had no idea what he was talking about, but he went on to say that it was my continuing to charge the dummy in bayonet drill without faltering or giving up that he used as the example. I was amazed.

When I arrived at West Point, I think I had shaved only once up to that point, and there was little indication of a beard on my unbelievably young face. While marching to and from Washington Hall, the massive mess hall, my youthful appearance drew unwanted attention from many upperclassmen. I was 17, but I looked about 14. I was continually stopped and asked, "Mister, how old are you?" The question implies, of course, that I should still be in high school and not in uniform at the nation's foremost military college. After many repetitions of this, I decided to take it on in a humorous vein by replying, "Sir, I am 17 and rapidly approaching puberty." That seemed to puzzle them even more, although some chuckled and found it creative and funny.

My brother's sketch of me as a fuzzy-cheeked Plebe

I had naively reported to the academy, carrying not only my suitcase but also a brand-new portable typewriter my parents had given me as a graduation present. This fact was discovered by the cadet company commander, who immediately made me his clerk, which meant typing a long report the same time each evening. Making it more onerous was the fact that you could not make duplicates. I had to make three originals with no errors or whiteouts. I therefore had to do this during the period when we were permitted to keep the lights on in our quarters, which meant I was unable to study. I began studying in the dimly lit corridors after taps, and my 20/20 vision in August became 20/200 by the end of my Plebe year. Hardly a way to create a fit, capable fighting man.

I was evidently congenitally predisposed to questioning authority and all that it portended, including keeping a tidy, immaculate locker full of underwear and other items neatly folded with paper inserts. I never really got the hang of that, nor did I think it in any way relevant to West Point's mission of producing combat leaders. The result of such indifference was that I was constantly given demerits for deficiencies in the more obscure areas of military discipline. Once one had more than the minimum demerits, one was required to walk (or rather march) punishment tours in the Central Barracks area on Saturday afternoons, one of the few periods when one was free to do something pleasurable, such as dating or reading in the library. Fortunately for me, visiting heads of state could grant amnesty, thus wiping out our punishment tours. To my great delight, Eisenhower was the president and frequently visited his alma mater. I was also saved by Princess Grace, King Mohammed V of Morocco, and Prince Albert of Belgium. Long live heads of state!

One of my more comical transgressions occurred as a result of my excelling in English studies. I routinely stood first or second in the class for the first six months or so. Plebes at that time marched their sections to class. I, being the leader of the first or ranking section of English students, was marching my section across Central Area in a rather haphazard manner, when the cadet officer of the day saw this undisciplined rabble and ordered me in stentorian tones to "halt those motherfuckers." I instantly turned to my worthy rabble and, in an equally stentorian voice, ordered, "Motherfuckers, halt!" The other Plebe marchers were convulsed with laughter, a reaction not evidently humorous to the cadet guards. I was accosted by the cadet guard and written up for insubordination.

There was then a hoary tradition that first-year cadets, plebes, would benefit in the mess hall by rotating each month to another table, headed by a different "table commandant." In September, I landed on the table of the first-classman, Ned Serio, a distinguished-looking Italian from San Francisco. I discovered right away that he had a highly ironic sense of humor, and I began playing to that. I researched jokes and riddles at the library and began plying him with them. He responded by letting my classmates and me eat "at ease" without the customary bracing. When it came time to change tables, Mr. Serio made the very unusual and controversial decision to take me with him. Soon, my classmates were vying to sit at my table since we were frequently relieved of the more onerous aspects of plebe life. It was through this experience that I decided my sense of humor was likely to be my saving grace in my remaining years at West Point.

One cool morning at reveille formation, I was standing at attention with my company when suddenly there was a great flurry of activity usually an indication that a high-ranking officer was approaching. It was, in fact, Lt. Gen. Blackshear Morrison Bryan, our superintendent, whose name I always thought was more appropriate for a Wall Street law firm. He approached me from behind, looked me over, and then asked, "Mister, may I touch you?" I, of course, said yes. He then began tugging at my body in a vain attempt to align it with my other company mates;

however, my scoliosis carried the day. Either my feet were aligned with the others, or my body. But never both at the same time. He then said, "This man has the most screwed-up posture of any cadet I've ever seen." I was secretly pleased since I'd finally excelled at something. I was promptly sent every Wednesday afternoon to "posture squad," a 2-hour torture session with the wrestling instructor, Mr. Kress. I was required to hang from an overhead bar for many minutes to stretch the muscles on my right side because of a low right shoulder. I startled Mr. Kress by making loud simian noises while hanging from the bar. The result is that I have a low left shoulder today.

Plebe year, I lived on the second floor in the South Area of barracks. On the first floor was another Plebe room. For some reason, I began spending time with the occupants of that room, including one William Stokes McDaniel. Billy, as I came to call him, was from Griffin, GA, had a year at Georgia Tech before entering West Point, and had a droll southern sense of humor. I also found him very attractive. Throughout the year, we became good friends despite our many differences in personality and experience. Unlike me, he was a natural in almost all aspects of cadet life, whether in studies, sports, or leadership. He ended Plebe year as a star man, the stars on his collar indicating that he stood in the top 10% of our class academically a high honor. He, however, in his typical fashion, was indifferent to this honor and attempted to avoid placing the stars on his uniform. At the end of the year, I asked him if he would like to room with me in our yearling (or sophomore) year, and he readily agreed.

My second year at West Point was fraught with many challenges. The most stressful was the news that my father had suffered an extremely serious heart attack and was hospitalized for a long period of time. The second was my increasing awareness that I was not "outgrowing" my homosexual bent, and living with Billy McDaniel only made that more apparent. I therefore realized that it was unfair to my girlfriend, Janie, to pretend otherwise, and I reluctantly terminated our longstanding relationship.

This disquieting setting also began to affect my studies to the point that my grades were falling precipitously. I had started out in Russian class doing remarkably well, but wound up at the very bottom of my section. The professor was Prince Podpalkovnic Leon Mirski, a relative of the Romanovs, who had been given an honorary commission as a Lieutenant Colonel in the US Army because his father had been a Field Marshal in the Imperial Russian Cavalry. He was commissioned into the Armor branch, which I found amusing because his hugely overweight body would never fit in a tank. He smoked outside the classroom until the very last moment when class was to commence. His uniform was then covered with the detritus from his cigarettes, giving him a kind of graceless charm. As I sank in my standing in his class, he would state in a loud Russian-accented voice, "I throw everyone out of the military academy, starting with Mr. Moss." I was always the dividing point in this disquisition. Having become enormously confused by all of this, I then seriously considered leaving the academy, but, realizing that this would be seen by my family as a failure on my part, I decided to stay, although without much enthusiasm.

My company mates quickly realized that, unlike most of them who came from middle- or lower-income families, my family was relatively well off and enjoyed a lifestyle very different from theirs. I was very impractical with finances, constantly having to borrow money from my classmates, which led me to be tagged "the poor little rich boy." I had all my civilian clothes made at Rogers Peet in New York and bought a gold Rolex watch. One weekend in New York, I bought a newly stylish outfit consisting of tan linen Bermuda shorts, a brown linen jacket, and matching argyle knee stockings. When I was getting dressed to prepare for a weekend in the city, wearing this rather unconventional outfit, my classmates lined the windows as I headed for the bus station, making loud, derisive hooting noises. I was a bit of a dandy, and it was not at all surprising that I was frequently without cash. Some years later, my father told me that my free education at the academy had cost him almost as much as Phil's five years at Hopkins all due to my profligacy. This, of course, led to other questions by my classmates, including whether I belonged at West Point at all. Each year, we were asked to rank our company mates on their military potential and leadership qualities. I was always dead last. *

*A quick ironic comment on this. I was unable to attend the first several West Point reunions because I was out of the country. My company mates in Company K-1 did very well in the military, with three of the 20 becoming general officers. However, when I made it to my first reunion in 1974, I was asked by my company mates, including the generals, to organize them and chair our mutual activities at the reunion. Thereafter, at every reunion, the man deemed unfit to lead others became the leader appointed by the generals.

Over my four years at West Point, I think I had a remarkably consistent effect on my various roommates, resulting in their sinking in class standing in most subjects. That was due to the fact that I was a disruptive roommate. I had a small record player and a stash of classical records, which I played frequently to the displeasure of all, who, unlike me, were raised with an aversion to classical music. Adding to my fascination with all things other than military discipline, I enjoyed reading the daily New York Times, which, to my astonishment, was left in each room in the morning. I very much enjoyed reading articles to my roommates, who were largely indifferent to the paper's contents. Thanks to my antics, Billy McDaniel, after his stellar first year, sank lower and lower in the academic ranks.

In the first several years, cadets were highly restricted in the time they could spend away from West Point, including weekends. As I recall, in the second year, we were permitted two trips. I always took the bus to New York City, where I indulged in activities not only different from what most typical cadets would have pursued but also probably repugnant to them. They included my fascination with the performing arts. I would buy standee tickets to the Metropolitan Opera for 75 cents and stand behind brass dividers for the entire opera. The standees, or claque, devotees, and typically besotted opera fans, were an especially charming and totally weird bunch. I felt right at home with them.

My second foray was to the ballet. At that time, I'd only read about classical ballet but had never attended a performance. I began with the Ballet Theater (later the American Ballet Theater), which was, and still is, one of the best companies in the world. I usually stayed at the Astor Hotel in Times Square, which then catered to cadets. My introduction to Italian cuisine came through dinners at Mama Leone's restaurant, where I first tasted prosciutto and melon. It would also seat cadets immediately, even if there were a long line waiting. I was beginning to feel like an adult.

Thus far, I have not said much about my education and learning. What struck me most and rather depressed me was that with one notable exception, no instructors or professors ever paid any attention to me. The one exception was an English teacher plebe year who was obviously impressed not only with my writing ability but also my knowledge of literature. He invited me several times to dinner with him and his wife. Unfortunately, that was his last year of assignment there. I probably made it somewhat difficult for the faculty by my increasing indifference to academics and by the very makeup of the academy's then-existing curriculum, which was almost 60% science and mathematics. In effect, during those four years I was educating myself through extensive reading on subjects not related to what was being taught. The one technical subject in which I excelled was Military Topography and Graphics, which had a large component of drawing and sketching.

I have alluded to my woeful physical abilities, which led to both serious and comical moments. The required physical education classes in the first year included boxing and wrestling. Boxing was taught by a man with the unlikely name of Punchy Kreaton. His approach was to teach us the basics and then to watch us duke it out; his criterion for success was quite simple if you bled during a bout or caused your opponent to bleed, you received a maximum score, whether or not this was done with skill or grace. I did both, and to my surprise, I was given a high grade. Later, I volunteered to box for my company's intramural boxing team and was probably more than a bit overconfident in my ability. My first opponent was my Filipino classmate, Pedro Baroidin, who was two inches shorter than I and had a reach several inches shorter than mine. In the very first round, he hit me with an uppercut, and I was knocked out cold, thus eliminating me from further competition.

I enjoyed wrestling and was rather good at it. One day during instruction, I was lucky enough to pin my opponent after a brief grappling session. It so happened that the upperclassman monitoring the class that day was from my company. On the way to lunch that noon, he announced my conquest as we marched to the mess hall and asked me in a loud voice which hold I'd used. My response was "Sir, I used a step over crotch hold." This, of course, caused great hilarity among the other marchers. My athletic limitations caused me to be shunted from one company intramural sport to another cross country, baseball and finally track. In the end, they gave up on me and made me a team assistant, responsible for toting equipment to events.

Another sport intensively taught in plebe year was swimming. They first gave us a swimming test in which we were asked to swim as far as possible in the pool during a timed period. I swam like crazy and made a remarkable number of laps. Based on this, they mistakenly placed me in the advanced swimming class. I knew right away that I was in the wrong group. They had us jump into the pool in khaki uniforms with an M-1 rifle. We were to remove our uniforms while floating, keeping the rifle aloft and then swim laps. I made the mistake of taking my shirt off using both arms at the same time, resulting in my arms being pinned behind me, and I thus began to drown. I was pulled out of the pool at the last minute and promptly reassigned to the beginner class.

One of my favorite stories from my less-than-awesome cadet career happened during one of my least favorite classes, mechanics of solids, taught by the formidable Major Frank Borman, later to be famed as an astronaut and the one who drove Eastern Airlines into bankruptcy. He took an instant dislike to me from the very outset. At that time, we used slide rules for our mathematical calculations. They had a hairline on both sides so that one could flip from one side to the other while working on a problem. I somehow had lost the glass hairline on my slide rule and had been operating it for many months using the aluminum edges, which I thought to be rather clever. Major Borman came up behind me while working a problem at the blackboards, noticed my missing hairline, and said in a loud voice, "Mr. Moss, you have no hairline," at which point I reached up to see if my actual hairline had unexpectedly receded. My classmates broke into great laughter when they saw my gesture. So, once again, I was written up for insubordination.

That same year, I volunteered to do something musical and, again, atypical. I was trained to be a "chapel chimer" in order to play the Anderson Carillon in the tower of the majestic protestant chapel.

**The Cadet Chapel and its great central tower with
the Anderson Carillon**

So, every Wednesday, I picked up the key to the chapel at the guard house, climbed the steep hill to the building, unlocked the door, went to the northwest tower, climbed the hundred or so steps to the walkway across the gothic vaulting below, and entered the central tower. Each evening, I played a number of standard hymns and West Point music, and at exactly 5 pm, I rang the hour. This meant I could skip the evening march to the mess hall and arrive for dinner at my leisure. On Sundays, if I were the designated chimer, I played a special concert before 11 am. Then I had to peer down an opening in the Gothic arch to see the organist 90 feet below, and when he placed his hand atop the console, it was my cue to play "West Point Peals" and then 11 o'clock on the bourdon bell. It also allowed me to take several trips to New York with the cadet choir. I loved it.

It was in my third year that I accomplished my greatest feat by defying the West Point norm, only to receive kudos for it. In the military leadership class, each cadet was to give a 15-minute talk or lecture to his classmates on a subject of his own choosing. In my class, most classmates spoke on excruciatingly boring subjects such as Napoleon's Prague maneuver, the tactics of Clausewitz or Moltke, or the history of the rifle. When it came my turn, the professor asked me, "Mr. Moss, what is your topic?" I responded, "Praxiteles and the development of naturalism in 4th-century BC Athenian sculpture." There was almost an audible gasp in reaction to such an absurd offering. The instructor appeared skeptical. I'd asked for various audio-visual aids in advance, which then allowed me to show my horny classmates dozens of photos of Praxiteles' famous nude female statues. My lecture went from being viewed with distain to being rapturously received. I had taken advantage of my classmates without them even knowing it. It was the only lecture that was asked to be repeated for other sections.

Billy McDaniel very quickly realized that although we were very close friends, my interest in him was both romantic and sexual. One weekend, we went together to the city and stayed at the Piccadilly Hotel. It was a hot spring day, and when we got to the room, he undressed in preparation for taking a shower. He was watching me while doing so, recognizing that my interest was more than casual. Then, when quite naked with just a towel over his shoulder, he stood in the middle of the room and said to me in his slow Georgian drawl, "You know, Marvin, it's a shame we're not both queer because we sure could have a lot of fun with each other." We both laughed while recognizing the potential seriousness of the situation.

Billy and Marvin, 1956

The last two years at West Point were very vexing for me. I'd spent a great deal of energy deflecting any indication of affection for Billy, and that effort seemed to have worked. Then, suddenly, in the middle of our junior year, he began distancing himself from me. It took me some time to understand that this was happening or to try to comprehend why it was occurring. He was dating an attractive young woman who lived in Fort Lee, NJ, at the time, and he seemed to be enamored of her. Only many years later did I realize that his distancing himself from me was an effort to protect not only himself but also me. Even in the absence of any sexual conduct, the very suggestion that a cadet had a crush on another was enough to send him home in disgrace to mama and papa. It was wise on his part to have done so, and in retrospect, I am very grateful.

The Soviet launching of Sputnik was especially memorable to me, possibly because it occurred on my 20th birthday, October 4, 1957. I realized immediately that this was certainly to be the impetus for a new and astonishingly expensive space race with major military implications. It was, of course, the basis for what turned out to be exaggerated claims in the 1960 presidential race of Soviet superiority in space and delivery systems.

A few months before graduation, I was in the 40th percentile academically of my class. Although I had great confidence in my ability, I realized my academic career had been influenced by a number of factors, including my dealing with my homosexuality, my indifference to many of the subjects we were required to take, and my lack of connection with most instructors. About 8 weeks before graduation, we all took the Graduate Record Examination. It was to be a two-hour exam. After the first hour, I got up to leave and was stopped by the officer proctor, who told me I had to remain for the balance of the time. I said, "I don't think that's necessary because I have just aced this exam." I was required to stay another hour.

Two weeks or so before graduation, I received a call from the Academic Dean's office asking me to come by the next day. No subject was given. My class was and is unique in many ways. The most obvious is that we had 6 Rhodes Scholars in the class, the largest number from a single college or university in the history of the program. I reported as ordered to the office of the Assistant Dean, a colonel, who was there with several full professors and department heads, the presence of whom indicated the potential seriousness of the meeting.

He began by saying, "Mr. Moss, we called you here because we are a bit mystified by you. 60% of your classmates outrank you academically. When we looked at your GRE scores, we were astonished. You had the third-highest score on the exam in your class, including besting four of the Rhodes Scholars. Our question to you is: How did this happen?" I knew I'd excelled in the exam, which is a true test of what you actually know rather than an attempt to gauge your intellectual potential. I thought for a moment and then said, "The GRE is a test largely unrelated to what you teach at West Point and is geared to people such as I who have been reading independently in the areas of social science and humanities for many years, including long before I came to West Point." At which point, one of them asked, "Can you give us an example of a question on the exam not related to our teaching?" Here is a good example, I said, "The question was what is the name of the final section of the first movement of a classical concerto involving improvisation by the soloist? The choices included: credenza, divertimento and cadenza. I've been listening to classical music since I was 6 years old, and I knew the correct answer was cadenza. I did not learn that here." It was obvious to me that none of them knew the answer to the question. I still have the report on my exam results. The class norm on all subjects was 1,588. My score was 1,770. I also told them I would have done fairly well on the GRE even when I graduated from high school, since I'd read widely in fiction, Shakespeare, and modern plays, and could identify much of classical music simply by hearing it. With puzzled looks on all their faces, I was dismissed. I left the room, realizing that I had once again stumped the West Point authorities and reveling in that thought.

**Graduation Photo a handsome,
confident, but somewhat skeptical man**

Two nights after our graduation, Billy and I rode in his sporty new red MG to a bar in nearby New Jersey and had drinks with lots of our classmates. We got quite drunk. On the way back, I lamented that we would probably not see each other for many years, since he was going into the Air Force. He suddenly pulled the car over to the side of the road and said, "Marvin, you are such an idiot. I do love you. You are the best friend I've ever had, but I can't love you the way you want me to." I was astounded and, of course, began crying.

On this unusual denouement of my cadet career, I left those hallowed halls with a sense that I'd entered West Point as a remarkably unusual person, had managed to confuse almost everyone about who I was for four years and left it questioning why I'd gone there in the first place. Despite my rocky journey, I have the greatest respect for West Point as an institution. Since I graduated, it has made almost unbelievably giant strides in modernizing the curriculum, establishing new majors and orienting cadets to the fact that modern warfare is fought in a manner that requires knowledge of the language, culture and a sophisticated understanding of other nations. I would have excelled in such a setting.

I look back now on my four years at West Point, perhaps a bit differently from many of my classmates, many of whom probably consider the academy the most important formative period in their lives, with an attachment to it that is incredibly strong. Although I now value that experience highly, I look on it more as an unusual launching pad for the life I've subsequently led. That said, I do believe that West Point continues to be not only a superb academic institution but also one that lives up to its mission. A speech President Theodore Roosevelt gave at West Point in 1902 addresses the importance of West Point from a national perspective. "Of all the institutions in this country, none is more absolutely American, none, in the proper sense of the word, more absolutely democratic than this. ...Here you come together as representatives of America in a higher and more peculiar sense than can possibly be true of any other institution in the land." I believe that was true in 1902 and still is today.

My entering West Point, fully aware that I was gay, was a rash, bold decision involving considerable trepidations about how I would survive for four years knowing my inclinations. It is only recently that I realized that perhaps my being gay and different was the source of many of the reactions of my classmates to me. Some, being wary of becoming too close to me for obvious reasons, were nonetheless intrigued by me and respected me because I was different. I was not aware of that at the time, and if I had been, I'm not sure how I would have reacted to that knowledge.

I would just point out that later in my life, as I entered new endeavors or organizations, I was ultimately chosen by participants to be their leader. That inherent leadership ability was never recognized by anyone at West Point except my long-suffering roommate, Billy McDaniel, who was fascinated by me, knew my potential, and had great confidence in my future professional life.

To this day, I do not know why I chose to go to West Point instead of Harvard or Dartmouth. Was I trying to prove something to myself, including that I could take the rigid physical and psychological challenges inherent in cadet life? Did I think I could somehow change or manage my homosexual desires (a neat trick in a place with 2,500 of the most fit and attractive men in the world)? I really do not know the answer to those questions. Another interesting question is, how did four years at West Point change me? Despite my outward appearance and reputation as a bon vivant (my company mates in Company K-1 dubbed me "the playboy of Kappa Uno"), * I was always a highly disciplined person even in high school. I think West Point honed in me the ability to accomplish a great many things quickly and well in a limited time attributes I still find useful today.

*Years later, at the retirement ceremony for my company mate and friend, Lieutenant General Jerry Hilmes, at Fort Myer, Virginia, at the reception in the officers' club after the parade, I was going through the receiving line. Jerry introduced me to his son, Andy, a recent West Point graduate who is now a retired general officer. As soon as he heard my name, he said, "You're Marvin Moss? I've been dying to meet you all my life. Mom and Dad have told me endless hysterical tales of your goings on at West Point and on leave in New York City."

Also, I sometimes wonder what would have happened if I'd attended Harvard or Dartmouth. I'd always had a keen interest in literature, writing, the arts in general, as well as architecture and history. Would I have become a success in one of those areas? Years later, when I was hanging out at the White Horse Tavern, Dylan Thomas' favorite West Village bar in New York, I did fantasize about becoming a bohemian poet living in a garret ala La Boheme. Who knows?

My high GRE scores were indicative of my early fascination with and interest in the arts. As I indicated to the West Point professors, much of my learning in that area came from independent reading over many years, including throughout high school. It is only now, in my twilight years, that I recognize what a great influence that interest has had on my life. Ralph Waldo Emerson believed that we consume culture to enlarge our hearts and minds. Or as David Brooks wrote in a recent article in the Times, "We gradually acquire more expansive ways of seeing the world… …but the humanistic mind expands outward to wider and wider circles of awareness."

I'm also startled now by how my perceptions of literature have changed over the years. In English classes at West Point, we were required to read Moby Dick. I found it boring and seemed oblivious to the poetry of much of the writing. Only years later, did I pick it up again and could not put it down. I'd been given a copy of Ulysses Grant's memoir as a graduation present, and after reading a few pages, abandoned it. Only years later, after reading some comments about what a masterpiece it was, did I return to it. It is indeed one of the great works of American literature. Perhaps, it is our own experience of life as we progress through time that enables us to see the beauty in some art and to appreciate it. For instance, I read The Brothers Karamazov only after becoming Orthodox and beginning to understand its theology. I don't think I would have understood much of it without having had that advantage.

Chapter 5
Germany 1959-1962

I was commissioned in the Signal Corps, the Army's communications arm, which was my first choice of branches. Among other things, I selected that branch knowing that many of its activities were with our forces stationed abroad, giving me a chance to continue learning about new lands, languages and cultures. After a few months of training at the Signal School in Fort Monmouth, NJ, I went to Fort Benning, Georgia, for paratrooper training. It is odd that after my relatively disastrous performance in athletics at the academy, I was in superb condition for this intense training.

Several funny incidents occurred while there. We had a very tall Black Military Police lieutenant in our group who was one of the most hilarious men I ever met. When we had to swing out from a platform in a parachute harness that passed between our legs, the lieutenant, as soon as he was launched, was screaming, "My balls, my balls." He was in the same aircraft with me during our first jump, and when the stick (the line of men about to jump) was ordered to leave the plane, he was in the door and yelled, "I ain't goin'." At which point the instructor booted him out the door. Also in my stick was my classmate, Willy Stocker, who was one of the smallest and lightest of cadets. He went out ahead of me, and when I landed at the rendezvous site, the instructor asked, "Where is Lt. Stocker?" I looked up, and there he was. He wasn't coming down. He was heading very rapidly toward the border with Alabama. Even today, I'm not sure how or where they finally found him.

On December 30, 1959, I flew from Dover Air Force Base with several of my classmates to my assignment with the US Seventh Army in Germany. We landed at Rhine Main Air Force Base on New Year's Eve. With my usual curiosity, I had been looking for things to do and see on the trip. So, I organized three of us to go into Frankfurt for dinner at one of Germany's most prestigious and elegant restaurants, the Kaiser Keller (it incidentally no longer exists). One of the classmates was my friend and company mate, Steve McSweeney. We were dressed in our formal dress blue uniform and greeted warmly by the maître d'. I'd brought with me my miniature English-German dictionary. When I noticed one of us was missing a napkin, I looked up the word and asked the waiter, "May we have a monat-spindel please?" He was nonplussed since I'd mistakenly just ordered a sanitary napkin. It was there that I first tasted the delicious Schildkrautensuppe, otherwise known as turtle soup laced with Madeira wine.

I was assigned to the 229th Signal Company in Böblingen, south of Stuttgart and on the edge of the Black Forest, with our base at Panzer Kaserne, the former headquarters of General Rommel. Our unit was responsible for important communications links between the 7th Army headquarters and its 5th and 7th Corps. Germany was at that time divided into three military sectors with the French near the Rhine Valley, the British in the north, and the US defending the central sector. A few days after my arrival, we departed for a major joint exercise in Bavaria named Winter Shield. My battalion and company were stationed in a densely wooded area near Regensburg. I loved these maneuvers because they gave me the opportunity to see some of the most beautiful towns and countryside in Germany, even though it was bitterly cold. Later, in a convoy to Bavaria for another exercise, I saw that all my trucks were, against my orders, pulling into an Army gas station between Ulm and Munich. I radioed my platoon sergeant and asked him what was happening. He said, "We're all going to meet Elvis, who is in his truck at the gas station." So, I got to shake his hand.

Our parent signal brigade had a gonzo, incompetent lieutenant colonel as its operations officer. We were living in tents heated by noisy contraptions with latrines alongside, as well as tubes for urinating. The colonel's preoccupation was that we were not using the tubes. He was constantly rebuking us for "making piss holes in the snow." One night in the tactical operations center, we suddenly experienced massive interference with our radio signals. The colonel demanded to know what was happening, and the duty lieutenant said it could be the aurora borealis, which was clearly visible in the sky. The colonel's response caused me to flee the tent in laughter since he said, "You tell those fucking Spaniards to get off our frequencies." The realization that senior officers could be crackers was quite a revelation.

One of my goals was to learn at least conversational German, so I began studying the language in evening and weekend classes provided on base and, relatively quickly, was able to communicate with the locals. I was surprised by how indifferent many of my classmates were to immersing themselves in the language and culture where we were to live for up to 3 years. One of my classmates frustrated me when we were again on maneuvers in Bavaria. One morning, he came to me, knowing I knew some German, and asked me where the village of Umleitung was, since he had seen signs for it everywhere. Umleitung, I had to explain to him, means detour. In the same conversation, I noted that the Donau River was thawing, and he responded to me, "I don't know about the Donau, but the Danube definitely is." I only shook my head.

When I was at West Point, my revered high school English teacher, Miss Rachel Sheetz, had gone to Hagerstown's German sister city, Wesel, to teach English for a year. She wrote me at school introducing me to an attractive young German lady, Christa Gunther, with whom I was corresponding regularly. I arranged to meet her in Cologne on the weekend. She was indeed as beautiful as her photos. She invited me to come to her hometown, Coesfeld in Munsterland, for Christmas. I did so, bringing Steve McSweeney along.

In 1960, I was first eligible to vote. The armed services had a relatively sophisticated system of allowing us to vote in statewide and national elections in absentia. During the 1960 campaign season, I was isolated from most US news coverage and got what news I did get from Stars and Stripes, the service newspaper, which was, of course, very non-partisan. I do know that in November 1960, I voted for Richard Nixon for president. I tell this only to illustrate my subsequent political odyssey.

On our way to Coesfeld, we drove to Hagerstown's sister city, Wesel am Rhein. I'd dedicated our 1955 Hagerstown High School yearbook to that mutual relationship. When we arrived, I called a friend of Rachel Sheetz, who then called the mayor and other city leaders. We wound up at the Rathaus, where we were introduced and warmly greeted by all, and ended our visit by joining the entire city staff in singing Christmas carols on the Rathaus steps. Steve was impressed. Christa introduced me to a fascinating friend of hers, General Terzic of Yugoslavia, who, with a dozen or so exiled monarchist officers, was living at Schloss Varlah, a beautiful castle near Munster. He had been the tutor of the last Yugoslavian king for many years. He spoke excellent English and German. He epitomized to me the old-world gentleman–sage, dignified and worldly. We had a wonderful visit and experienced a typical traditional German Christmas celebration.

Marvin, Christa and General Terzic at Castle Varlah

I later took her with me to learn to ski in the Tyrolean Alps at Lech. We both learned the rather exaggerated local style of skiing fairly quickly. We were staying at a traditional farmhouse above the village, which could only be reached by taking a T-bar lift and skiing down to it. On New Year's Eve, we went to the very elegant and exclusive local hotel, the Berghof, for dinner and the midnight celebration. This hotel was known for the celebrities who routinely stayed there, including the Dutch royal family and Hugh O'Brien (aka Wyatt Earp) and his then-girlfriend, the exiled former Empress of Iran, Farah Diba. So, we were in exalted company. At our table were a Dutch family and the president of Pan Am Airways, Najeeb Halaby, and his family, including his daughter, Lisa, who later became Queen Noor of Jordan. We had a great time, although we were the only paupers at the table. In an odd note, many years later in Washington, DC, my Palestinian friend, Dr. Nuha Abudabbeh, became a close friend of the exiled Queen Noor.

Marvin and the stunning Christa are soaking up the sun in Lech

I was exploring Germany and Switzerland regularly on extended weekends when we were not in the field or on alert status, which was fairly common in those Cold War days. On one trip with Steve McSweeney in my little brown VW, we drove to Zurich and stayed at the Eden au Lac Hotel, a gorgeous place overlooking the Zurichersee. The staff, seeing our beat-up car and our casual clothes, looked askance at us, but with an exchange rate very favorable to the dollar, we were able to live it up on our measly Army salary. Many years later, during a stay in Zurich, I returned to the Eden au Lac for cocktails only to discover that rooms there started at $800 a night. How ironic that we stayed there in 1960 on a salary of $220 a month and in 2015 could only afford a cocktail.

In December 1961, 13 second lieutenants at Panzer Kaserne were promoted to first lieutenant, so I decided to organize a promotion party in the ballroom of the officers' club, which had evidently been made quite elegant when Rommel was in residence there. I hired a Bavarian oompah band for our dancing, had an open bar, invited all the post's officers and their wives and served a buffet dinner. Things got exciting when my bachelor officer quarters suite mate took my VW bus to Stuttgart to the Drei Farben Haus, the government-run and inspected brothel, filled the bus with the most attractive prostitutes and launched them on the dance floor. By that time, an unpredicted blizzard began outside, and most officers and wives were already fairly potted. The oompah band was especially drunk. I threw open the French doors to the balcony around midnight, and it was now snowing in the ballroom. People were dancing and singing; single officers were picking up the prostitutes; and I was dancing with Hildegarde, the wonderful but quite overweight waitress. In doing the waltz with her, I almost cast her out the open French doors into the blizzard. I was delirious with the madness of it all. My classmate, Steve McSweeney, who was one of the promoted lieutenants, recalls that there was so much snow in the ballroom that a snowball battle took place. Around 3 am, the band played its last lonely toot. As I closed the door, I sang the last line of Pagliacci, "la comedia e finita." Needless to say, I was called on the carpet on Monday morning for organizing what was, by then, being called an orgy.

The Soviets began building the Berlin Wall in August 1961 and shut down the rest of Soviet controlled Eastern Europe's access to the West. The reaction on the part of the 7th Army was quick and dramatic, resulting in my outfit spending months at a time in the far eastern reaches of Bavaria along the Czech border. This gave me an opportunity to explore an area of Germany I had never seen before, including the Hoch Hopfenstrasse, the area where most of the hops used to produce beer were grown. I also had an opportunity to visit frequently with the French troops there, who, with typical Gallic foresight and gastronomic priorities, were staying in snug gasthauses and stone barns with an enormous stack of red and white wine bottles.

Our living arrangements at Panzer Kaserne were interesting. Unmarried officers lived in the BOQ (bachelors officers' quarters); however, this particular building also contained two floors of mostly female schoolteachers who taught at the base school an interesting combination. There was much socializing between the two groups, and we frequently gathered at the officers' club bar in the early evening. I was very popular with both groups and known for my offbeat sense of humor and spirit of adventure.

Despite my happy times with my many friends, I always had a yearning sense of underlying sadness in my life. Why? I was never quite sure. Perhaps it was the dawning realization that, without a true love, my life was destined to be lived on the surface. Down the road from the BOQ was an old Wachtturm (watchtower) from World War Two. In it was a small wurst and beer stube run by a taciturn, laconic veteran of the Eastern Front. I would sneak away to it sometimes late in the evening, making sure no one was coming with me, sit in the rusting chairs overlooking the adjacent village, and drink a schnapps or a beer and contemplate my life. The Ober left me completely alone. I cherished those moments of solitude, although these excursions never resolved the underlying riddle of my discontent.

One weekend, a group of friends, including teachers, officers, and me, took off for Garmisch-Partenkirchen at the foot of the Zugspitze, Germany's highest mountain, for a skiing excursion. One of the friends was Ingrid Neuse, whose father was a professor of German at Middlebury College, and she was captain of the women's ski team. She was, of course, fluent in German. We took the cog railroad up to the summit to ski in the bowl. On the way down in the train, she convinced me to get off at a mid-station called Tunnelfenster (the tunnel window) and ski back to our hotel from there. Although I was a competent skier, I hadn't realized what lay ahead. The descent was almost completely vertical. It took me over two hours to get to the bottom, and by the time I got there, my wool sweater was completely covered in the back with a large chunk of ice. I was exhausted. I went into the men's room at the hotel to get the ice off, and there at the urinal to my astonishment was none other than Billy McDaniel. We greeted each other, and he helped me get the ice off my sweater.

I then invited him to join us for dinner at a nearby traditional restaurant. Our gang of about 6 was already well into our beers and beginning to act accordingly when Billy arrived. After introductions, he sat with us. I think he was surprised at how easily I was conversing with the waiters and Ingrid in German. After we ordered, I was observing him. I realized that it was difficult for anyone to be thrust into a group of people you did not know, but I saw, or perhaps I imagined, that he was a bit astonished at how much fun our group was having and how I seemed to be the center of the action. I think he felt a bit out of it. He was stationed temporarily at that time at the Wiesbaden Air Force Base, where he had just arrived, and I had the impression from that evening that he was quite lonely. When he left, we hugged and exchanged contact information. I felt it was a very strange and sad reunion.

At Panzer Kaserne, I commanded what was probably the largest platoon in Germany almost 200 men. Our mission was to provide telephone and radio communications for the 7th Army, a vital role during those trying times. I had a wonderful Black platoon sergeant, Sergeant Gibson, who kept me on the straight and narrow most of the time. The result was that I frequently had communications rigs stationed across central Germany, from the Czech border to the Rhine. I was therefore provided with a helicopter to fly from place to place. One day at a rig in Bavaria, I was inside it and picked up the order wire (an administrative connection linking various communications rigs). When I picked it up, I heard one of my troops asking, "Is Mighty Mouse at your location?" When I got back to base, I asked Sergeant Gibson who Mighty Mouse was, and he chuckled and replied, "You are Mighty Mouse, sir." He assured me it was meant as a compliment. I took his word for it. During all of this, my commanding officer was Captain Richard W. Smartt (with two tt's as he always said). He was a great commander and an admirer of my work. He wrote an efficiency report on me that suggested I be raised to the rank of general as quickly as possible. He also played an important role in my life later as I was departing Vietnam.

The final saga of Germany is of two wonderful trips taken with friends and my parents. The first was with Steve McSweeney and friends from Hagerstown: Martha Stoner, Rosemary Torrine, Joanne Mullendore, and Don Frank. We took off in my camper bus to Munich, then through the high Grossglockner Pass in Austria, to Venice, and on to Florence. Rose Mary's mother was a cousin of the Contessa Maria Louisa Fabiani, who owned a hotel in Florence, so we stayed there and had a delightful traditional Tuscan dinner with her and her husband, Count Fabiani. On the way back, we visited Zermatt and the Matterhorn, where I ate artichokes for the first time in my life. It was a grand trip.

The next year, 1962, my parents came to Germany to visit with another Hagerstown couple, Landis and Kitty Coffman. Landis owned the largest lumber company in Western Maryland and was quite wealthy. They also happened to be great characters with a sense of adventure. I picked them up in Bingen along the Rhine River, where they arrived on a steamer. My father, who had now had a series of heart attacks, was still as jolly as ever and kept referring to the attractive young German women as "froolines." My father was essentially an uneducated man, having attended evidently only the first grade. He had little knowledge of the world despite marrying a woman who was much more sophisticated. When we arrived in Venice at the parking garage and took the vaporetto to Piazza San Marco, Dad was standing next to me. He looked at me and asked, "Bud, you mean there are no streets here?" I suddenly realized he had no clue what Venice was, but I saw that he was soaking it all in and enjoying the beauty and splendor of what he was seeing. Watching his reaction, I had tears in my eyes.

One of my friends at our base was Helen Ludwig, a school teacher who was an amazing character intelligent, witty, audacious and slightly bizarre. We in the BOQ christened her "Mad Ludwig" after Ludwig II, the almost certainly gay mad king of Bavaria, who was smitten with Richard Wagner. Nine months before I was scheduled to return to the States, a new teacher arrived Woody. Woody had been captain of his high school and college wrestling teams and looked it. He was short, about 5ft. 6in, with a perfect male body, which he emphasized by wearing tight pants and open shirts. He was incredibly sexy. I knew instantly that he was gay, and he knew instantly that I was attracted to him, a fact I believe he conveyed to Mad Ludwig. I had fantasies of escaping with him to my favorite little hotel in the Black Forest for a weekend, but alas, it never happened.

In the late summer of 1962, I received orders to return to the States for the advance course at the Signal School at Fort Monmouth, NJ. I decided to return in the most unusual way possible. I requested to return on a troop ship so that I could experience the high seas once again. I took the train to Bremerhaven, and we sailed from there. The troop ship, the USNS Gordon, was a World War II vintage vessel. Officers on board were in quarters only slightly better than those of the enlisted men, with bunks stacked to the ceiling. I organized a bridge club. I was also assigned to be one of the officers in charge of the enlisted quarters. Everything went fine until we entered the North Sea, where we encountered the typical storms and high seas. My troops in the hold were almost to a man seasick, so I was spending a great deal of time ensuring that they remained as healthy as possible under the circumstances.

After landing at La Rochelle, France, to pick up another unit, we sailed directly to New York. It was on the ship that I read in the Army Times that the Army was launching a new graduate program, the Foreign Area Specialist Training (FAST) program, with a focus on sub-Saharan Africa. I decided to apply as soon as I could get to Washington. From there, I went to Hagerstown for a few weeks of home leave. In many ways, I regretted leaving Germany, where I'd excelled at my work, learned a new language and had used it as a base to explore much of Europe.

My almost 3 years in Germany were powerfully formative ones for me. Among other things, I discovered I could command a large group of men from diverse backgrounds and help them function as a cohesive unit. In their eyes, Marvin Moss had become Mighty Mouse. I also learned that our non-commissioned officers actually ran the Army despite our pretense of being the leaders. I'll never forget an incident that involved my Black platoon sergeant, the invaluable Sergeant Gibson. I was sitting in my office when a young Black GI I'd reprimanded for neglecting his duties came into the office and began telling Sergeant Gibson that Lt. Moss was a racist. Sgt. Gibson listened calmly for a few minutes and then bellowed to the cowed GI, "Lieutenant Moss is one of the fairest men I've ever met in my life. You are a slacker and a sad sack of a soldier. Now get out of here, and if I hear you say anything like this again, you will be in the brig." Much of that, or course, was said for my benefit, but I thanked him and told him how much I appreciated his loyalty and his peerless ability to keep our troops in line.

Perhaps the most important aspect of this period is my deep dive into German and continental culture. I attended the opera and ballet in Stuttgart regularly and heard the Czech Philharmonic perform Beethoven's Ninth Symphony in a concert where their formal attire was in tatters, bringing tears to my eyes in the finale when the chorus sings of "Freiheit," or freedom. I attended a concert in the throne room of Schloss Ludwigsburg by Van Cliburn soon after he'd won the prize in Russia. I became proficient in German to the point that my friend Christa Gunther was writing all her letters to me in German.

I'd traveled throughout Germany, Holland, Switzerland, France, Austria and Italy while attempting to learn as much as possible through those trips. I'll never forget my brief trip to France, where other officers and I were flown to Paris in a military transport. Halfway to Orly, one of the engines stopped, and we were told to put on our parachutes (I think I was probably the only trained paratrooper on board). Fortunately, we made it safely. Once at Orly, the pilot deliberately parked our small aircraft in front of the nose of a huge Soviet military plane, thus blocking it. I took the Metro into the city, sat in a café in the Left Bank, a femme de la nuit came and sat opposite me, and Marvin got totally spooked.

This was also the period of heightened potential conflict with the Soviet Union and the construction of the wall, thus isolating the East Germans. I wanted to visit Berlin throughout this period, but I was blocked because, at that time, one had to travel in a military convoy through East Germany and the Soviet Zone. Since I held the highest security clearances, I was not permitted to go. My unit in 1962-1963 spent endless months camped on the frontier with East Germany and Czechoslovakia. We were almost constantly on a high alert status and unable to be away from our units for any length of time.

Germany in 1960, just 15 years after the end of the war, was already experiencing its incredible Deutsches Wirtschaftswunder, the economic miracle. Stuttgart had removed all the debris from the bombing, collected it in one huge pile near the city center, and very creatively turned it into a new park. The city was attractive and immaculately clean. The nearby Mercedes and Porsche factories were already going full tilt. Food was plentiful (much of the Army's milk and other food then came from Holland and Denmark). The Germans I met regularly were fond of Americans and very supportive of our military presence.

Having lived in Germany for so long, I was, of course, curious about how the Volk viewed the war. Ferreting that out was done only with great difficulty since inquiries were generally met with silence or obfuscation. I learned not to press the point. In an odd way, it was almost as if the war had not taken place. And yet, in the end, I sensed that there was an overarching sentiment among the Germans that they needed to put in place a government that would make what happened in the 1930's impossible in the present. The Chancellor throughout my tour was the great Konrad Adenauer, who initiated both the Wirtschaftswunder and the nascent stirrings of a European common market. His legacy was later brilliantly extended by Willy Brandt from 1969-1974, who also reached out to the Soviets and began an early effort to stabilize relations with East Germany. Germany was very blessed to have such great leadership at such a crucial time.

Chapter 6
The Schooling Years

Reading my mother's letters many years later, I could see that she and my father were still holding out the hope that I would leave the Army and return to Hagerstown. I tried as diplomatically as I could to disabuse them of that notion. Dad was now chronically ill from his angina heart disease, and they were spending time at Mass General and Hopkins consulting with experts in a futile effort to ferret out a cure, which in those days simply did not exist. Phil had reluctantly agreed to come home and assist with the insurance business, a true sacrifice on his part.

I was one of the youngest and most junior officers in the advanced course. The first day, we were given a long examination in map reading, one of the few subjects at West Point in which I excelled. I left the exam early again, raising eyebrows among my fellow officers. The next day, it was announced that I was the only one to get 100% on the exam, adding to the aura of mystery that was beginning to surround me. It was a lonely time. Most of the officers in the course were married and lived off base, including my former West Point roommate and friend, Jim Dorsey. I lived in the BOQ on base.

I then started going to New York almost every weekend, spending time attending the opera, ballet, and Broadway plays. I also began, for the first time, exploring the gay bars in the West

Village, finally finding my home away from home at Julius, one of the oldest and seediest hangouts. It was during a performance of Aida at the Met that I was among the standees, when a young man, a dwarf, came in and was standing behind me. Concerned that he could not see, I let him stand in front of me. While the soprano was singing the great aria, "ritorna vincitor," the young man reached back and firmly grasped my genitals. I gently removed his hand. He fled at the intermission and never returned. My parents had warned me of the many perils that could lie ahead in life, but never that a dwarf gay man at the opera could accost me. In those days at the old Met on West 39th Street, the orchestra during intermissions would dash across the street to an Irish bar and slug down drinks. I always went with them. Their playing inevitably deteriorated as the evening wore on, especially if the opera had multiple intermissions, such as in Wagner's Götterdämmerung. In that opera, at the very end, the gods hardly got immolated due to the orchestra's errant fiddling.

It was also the time of the Cuban Missile Crisis, which I was monitoring every evening on the one television set in my quarters. It was, of course, difficult to know exactly what was really happening from the press coverage, and it was only many years later, when the actions of President Kennedy were revealed, that it became clear how threatening it had been and how cleverly he handled it.

My class was at Fort Lee, Virginia, on a logistics training exercise in May of 1963. Jim Dorsey and I were having drinks at the Officers Club when the duty officer came in. He announced that my mother was trying to get in touch with me because my father had died that day. Despite the fact that he'd been desperately ill for many years, I was still shocked. I took a bus to DC, where Uncle Marvin met me and took me to Hagerstown for the funeral. After the funeral, I was very worried about our mother's future not financially but emotionally, since I knew she was the kind of person who needed someone around her to love. Soon thereafter, I was at an art cinema in New York when a short documentary came on with Dylan Thomas reciting his poem "Do not go gentle in that good night." He had written it to commemorate his father's death, and I was so moved in light of Dad's recent death that I subsequently memorized the poem. Years later, after reading about Thomas' life, I started hanging out at the White Horse Tavern in the Village pretending that I was a great artist or poet (and ignoring the inconvenient fact that it was there that Thomas drank himself to death).

In the summer of 1963, I was enrolled at The American University in Washington in its new program of African studies, a graduate program of the US Army. The class consisted of about 9 Army officers and several civilians, including Barbara Wilson and Joseph Pegues, who later became lifelong friends. The principal course was a seminar headed by Dr. Darrell Randall, who had been a missionary in Africa. I was also taking other courses, including an intensive French course taught by a very attractive young French woman, Madame de Jong. I picked it up fairly quickly despite my difficulty with the subtlety of the vowel sounds, which tended to elude a native of Western Maryland, where all vowel sounds are exactly the same.

While at the university, I lived in an inexpensive one-bedroom apartment on Wisconsin Avenue near the National Cathedral, where I frequently studied on warm days in its beautiful gardens. Late that summer, I received a letter from Billy stating that he'd left the Air Force and was returning home to Georgia to work in his father's insurance firm. He came to visit me for several days, staying at my apartment. I was just as attracted to him as before. He seemed to enjoy being with me and seeing my new life in a very different setting. After he left, he would call me fairly frequently, resulting in long, soulful conversations that led me to conclude he was still lonely and frustrated. He was being much more candid with me than ever before. I also sensed that our friendship and love for each other would endure.

Billy married a few years later and invited me to be part of the wedding party, which I declined because of my lingering feelings for him. Soon thereafter, I met his wonderful wife, Martha. We started going to West Point reunions together and had a great time travelling to and from West Point. We shared common interests in gardening, travel, history and public service. At our last reunion in 2009, when both were present, I was sitting with Martha just the two of us. I asked her what she thought attracted Billy to her in the first place, and she, being fully aware of the long-standing mutual love between Billy and me, responded, "It's really quite simple, Marvin. In me, he finally found a female version of you." We both laughed. Unfortunately, they are both now dead, and I miss them terribly.

On November 22, 1963, I was napping in my apartment before going to afternoon classes. I walked out of the apartment and immediately encountered a young man on the sidewalk who was weeping. He told me about President Kennedy's assassination. Once it was clear that he was to be buried at Arlington after a funeral mass at St. Matthew's Cathedral, I called my mother and Phil and asked them if they wanted to come join me in honoring the president. Steve McSweeney, who at that time was stationed at Fort Ritchie near Hagerstown, also wanted to come along. We stood on Connecticut Avenue near the cathedral as the cortege went by, including many crowned heads of Europe, Charles de Gaulle, Haile Selassie and so many others. It was a very emotional day; one I shall never forget. Afterwards, we went to a quiet and solemn lunch at one of my favorite Georgetown restaurants, Billy Martin's Tavern, where JFK had proposed to Jackie.

In early 1964, Dr. Randall announced that the class was scheduled to take a long, well-planned trip to Africa to round out our studies. I found the prospect very exciting doubly so since many of the former colonies had recently become independent or were in the process of doing so. Despite some reservations I had about Dr. Randall's academic qualifications and teaching style, I had to admire his tenacity and imagination in putting together a trip that was from the outset going to be a monumental undertaking. The officers in the class and Barbara Wilson were to be on the trip with us.

Chapter 7
The African Awakening

We left in May, flying first to London, where arrangements had been made for us to meet with senior officials at the Ministry of Foreign Affairs, and then on to Paris. In Paris, we were again wined and dined by government officials with experience in the French colonies. It just so happened that Joe Pegues, our friend from university in Washington, was studying in Paris at the time and was becoming fluent in French. Also, my dear friend, Mad Ludwig from Germany, was to meet me there. I led the three of us on a memorable, utterly unforgettable foray into la vie française. We started around 10 pm with after-dinner drinks, then visited the giant al fresco Les Halles central market, strolled the streets and finally began a tour of the tiny bistros in the neighborhood, all the while becoming more and more intoxicated by lively spirits and our own joie de vivre. When I headed back to the hotel, the sun was coming up.

Then on to Lisbon. There, the situation was very different, in that the Portuguese had been and were then disinclined to countenance any glimmer of their colonies' hopes for independence. We were treated royally with dinner, tours and lectures. Our Foreign Ministry escort was a very suave, handsome young count, who quickly had the women in our group firmly in his grasp.

We flew from Lisbon to Senegal, where, to my astonishment, I was asked to meet its president, the great French scholar Leopold Senghor. He was an accomplished French poet, a proponent of "negritude," which honored African writing and culture, and, finally, one of the first Africans elected to the Académie française. I can only imagine what he thought of my fractured French. Our next stop was Accra, Ghana, where we stayed at the university, then one of a series of first-rate African universities in the English-speaking former colonies associated with the University College of London. The others were the University College of Rhodesia and Nyasaland, the University of Ibadan, Nigeria, and Makerere College in Kampala, Uganda. In each case, final examinations were graded locally and then sent to London for a second review. Standards were very high at all of them. We met with students and faculty at the university and learned a great deal, including interest in the relatively newly revised concept of Pan-Africanism. We had a unique experience in Accra. It happened that we were eating our evening meal in the university's al fresco dining room when the annual termite swarm brought thousands of them into the lighted rooms, where they instantly dropped their wings into our soup bowls.

Arrangements had been made for us to travel from Accra to Ibadan, Nigeria, by bus. I'd been a bit concerned from the outset of the trip that the group's cohesion might be illusory and ephemeral, given the unusual composition of my fellow travellers; military professionals whose trip was being paid for by the government and civilians who were footing their own expenses. In addition, there were only two Black officers in the group and one African, Fred Njenga from Kenya. Most Army officers were very conservative politically, as were most commissioned officers at the time. This was, of course, the apogee of the violence associated with the civil rights movement in the United States. I, and one other officer, Captain Daniel Mark Collier, a Harvard graduate, were, on the other hand, more progressive in our thinking. I was correct to worry about this, as subsequent events and some awkward situations demonstrated.

We boarded what looked to be a relatively modern bus in Accra, driven by a neatly uniformed African driver. For some reason, Barbara and I decided to sit in the back seat. We'd gone perhaps only 15 miles or so when the exhaust pipe, just below a large hole in the back of the bus, began spewing toxic fumes into the bus. I then went to Dr. Randall and protested that we would all be dead by the time we reached our destination. He had the driver return to Accra. We unloaded everything and eventually got a new and less lethal bus. We transited Togo and Dahomey on the way, skirting the sea as we went.

Finally, we reached the Nigerian frontier where a major and unanticipated contretemps ensued. It seems the new bus driver had not been given the proper documentation to allow the bus to enter Nigeria. At one point, we were close to being ordered to return from whence we'd come already a dusty and rather uninteresting trip. I really never found out how this was resolved, but given the Nigeria of the time, I'm quite sure money was involved. After a long delay, we were again on our way. The area of Nigeria we were now travelling through had been pummeled by a major storm in the last few days, and all the streams were overflowing their banks. Finally, we arrived at a river with a rickety, old, narrow wooden bridge across it, the river surging just below the structure. The bus stopped. We looked at the situation, and I suggested that we unload all the luggage from the bus to lighten it and have all the passengers walk across the bridge with several remaining on board to help guide the very frightened driver maneuver across the span. This was the first split in the group. None of the brave officers volunteered to stay in the bus, so Barbara, Fred Njenga and I elected to do so. We were hanging out the front windows as we carefully coached the driver across. I will never forget the raging torrent as we got to the middle. Fortunately, we made it safely. Finally, we were on our final leg to Ibadan.

Although I knew very little about traditional African tribal art, I was purchasing some interesting items as we went along, including some early pieces from the Senufo Tribe in the Ivory Coast. Traditional art from this area of West Africa, with its exaggerated and elongated figures, had played an important role in influencing early 20th-century European art, including that of artists such as Giacometti. In my collection is this leopard on the mantel in my great room a superb example of the Senufo style.

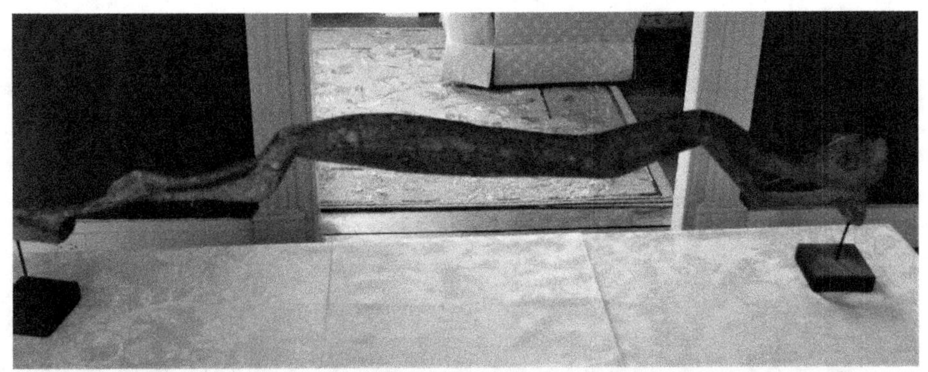

In Ibadan, we met Uli Beier, a German expatriate, who, with his wife, had founded an atelier called the Oshogbo School, specializing in traditional and new forms of art in all media from the Yoruba Tribe. It was from him that I purchased this divination bowl with its cast bronze heads, which now resides in my dining room. It is one of my favorite African pieces.

Yoruba Divination Bowl

Detail of the Divination Bowl showing the bronze heads cast by the lost wax process (cire perdue)

Beier had a strong interest in African literature as well and founded a new literary journal, Black Orpheus, which began publishing the works of unknown but later acclaimed writers, including Chinua Achebe and Wole Soyinka, the Nobel laureate, both from Nigeria. The Ibadan University was impressive in almost every way. We had a productive stay there, including many meetings and discussions with students and faculty.

We next flew to Luanda, the capital of Angola, Portugal's East African colony. I was surprised how Portuguese it actually was. It was an attractive seaside city, with its government buildings reflecting Lisbon's architecture and style. The climate was moderate year-round, and when we met with the US Consulate staff, one of the young diplomats described it as "the Foreign Service's best kept secret." There may have been some inklings of the chaos that was to ensue in later years as the indigenous population struggled toward independence; however, we were perhaps naively unaware of it. My small group, including Dan Collier, was having drinks on the rooftop terrace of a café when a young American Peace Corps volunteer arrived, and we asked him to join us. When introductions were made, and he heard Dan's name, he said, "You are Johnny Slive." We had no idea what he was talking about until he explained that Dan was notorious among recent Harvard grads as the author of a roman a clef entitled "Love with a Harvard Accent," in which the main character, Johnny Slive, was a pimp. Instantly, Dan became Johnny Slive.

From Luanda, we took a memorable flight across all of central Africa on a Constellation. Memorable in what we were seeing out the windows on this seemingly endless flight. Frequently, on both sides of the plane, you could see vast areas of the savannah on fire around the Okavango Delta, the largest inland delta in the world, created by the annual flooding of the Okavango River into the normally desiccated Kalahari Desert. These fires were either deliberately set by the Herrero or other indigenous people in their very clever attempt to fertilize the land for their cattle herds or by lightning. It was both beautiful and a bit terrifying.

It was at this point in our journey that I began keeping a daily diary of our passage through some of the most interesting places imaginable. Looking back on that document now, I am a bit chagrined at some of my writing since it smacked of both hubris and insensitivity. It, however, does provide an accurate record of where we were and what we were doing, as well as a list of many of the important governmental and academic people we met. Much of what follows is based on my diary.

Our stay in Lorenzo Marques, the capital of Mozambique, was not as interesting as our stay in Angola. We received little attention from US authorities, and there was no university for us to approach students and faculty for discussions about the country and its future. I did remark that I would miss the wonderful Portuguese cuisine and that I was dreading the return to English bland vegetables boiled to the point of oblivion. In early August, we flew from there to Salisbury, Rhodesia.

Knowing that I was slated to return to Salisbury later on my own, I was paying special attention to the university and to what was happening in the country at the time. We were hosted by the university and stayed in its dormitories. The very first night, I invited a group of students and faculty members to my room, which led to a broad discussion of the current political situation with Ian Smith and his government. Included in the group were Dr. Andrew Brock, a physicist; an Indian student; and Byron Hove, an openly gay African student who had been elected President of the prestigious Student Union (this fact was in itself an eye-opener). The next day, after a guided tour of the relatively depressing townships surrounding Salisbury, I organized a dinner with Dan, Barbara, Marla Bush (a student on our trip), Godfrey Savanhu, an African student and son of one of the first African junior ministers, and Fred Njenga. I hosted them at Miekle's Hotel, the city's only first-rate hotel. I was beginning to understand that I could possibly become a part of the student body in a way that would facilitate my studies there.

In the following days, while attending lectures, I met Judith Todd, a student and the daughter of Sir Garfield Todd, the former Prime Minister who was defeated by his party caucus for advocating increased enfranchisement of minority voters. Later, she became one of my closest friends. Our seminar hosted an evening reception for all university students, with a large turnout from all groups. Two of the professors I met that evening were Sir Charles Cummings (the principal of the university) and Dr. Kingsley Garbett, professor of social anthropology. Sir Charles was later to become my bete noire during my next incarnation there.

In 1964, Rhodesia was a leading producer of tobacco, an important part of its economy and export earnings. Most of the tobacco farms were enormous, covering up to 1,000 acres and employing countless African laborers. On our itinerary was a visit to the tobacco auction outside Salisbury. It was early in the morning. The White staff there served us coffee, including the two Black officers, but refused to serve our African colleague, Fred Njenga. Fred was not at all surprised, given the then-current state of race relations in Rhodesia, but the Black officers were furious. We were to leave on a bus tour of the country, and they initially refused to go. I don't know how they thought we could rectify this situation, and eventually, they agreed to come along with us.

The university was full of colorful characters, many of whom I grew to love in my subsequent stay. On the last night, three totally whacky students (I dubbed them the three stooges) knocked on the door of Major David Parker, one of our most conservative officers, and, when he answered, they asked, "Would you like a girl, sir?" He said no and slammed the door. A few minutes later, they were back and asked, "Well then, how about a little boy?" Again no. In the final onslaught, they offered Major Parker a goat. They proceeded to lampoon American politics, which they obviously knew well, by deploring the rise of communism in the States and passing out John Birch Society pamphlets. Needless to say, I invited them to my room for a chat.

The seminar group then took off in a very modern bus replete with bar, piped music and a loo, a complete contrast from our last bus. We were headed into a fascinating area of eastern Rhodesia bordering Mozambique. Our goal was the frontier town of Umtali and the neighboring Chimanimani Mountains. Umtali had the appearance of a movie set for a spaghetti western. Its main street was enormously wide because it was founded in the days when the means of transportation were ox carts, which needed a lot of space to turn. We crossed the Chimanimani River and entered the mountain range with its glorious scenery and barren hills towering above us, capped by luminous clouds. There were small farms, isolated deep in the valley floors, oddly enough, causing me an unexpected sense of nostalgia for our 18 acres in Western Maryland.

On the second day, we traveled through the isolated village of Melstetter on our way to the great classical ruins of Zimbabwe. It was at the Zimbabwe Ruins Hotel where we had our second major crisis in the group. The Black officers and Fred were not permitted to stay at the hotel. Several of us discovered that the hotel had a series of charming thatched-roof cottages on its grounds. We suggested that all of us move into the cottages, which evidently lacked the hotel's racial restrictions. We did so, bringing a semblance of peace to the group. I was stunned the next day when the Black officers, incensed at their treatment the night before, refused to go on the tour of the ruins, one of the great classic sites of African culture. The logic of their position escaped me.

The Zimbabwe ruins are unique, with no equivalent in the rest of Africa as far as I know. It was built by a sophisticated society with an evidently inherent understanding of how to integrate a monumental structure into its surroundings. It has a fascinating history, albeit a mysterious one. It was evidently built from the 9th to the 15th Centuries as the administrative center of a tribal kingdom—perhaps the precursor of the current Shona people who now live in the area. It covers an area of 2.8 square miles and, at one stage, had a population estimated at about 18,000. To illustrate the colonial attitudes toward its African population, Rhodesia for many years denied the possibility that African natives could have built such an extensive city built of stone without mortar. We climbed up the ancient ascent to the acropolis affording a wonderful view of the countryside and the rest of the ruins. That evening, we invited Edward, our African driver, to join us for dinner in our cottage and before a roaring fire, we plied him with questions about his understanding of the situation in Rhodesia. It was one of the most memorable days of our trip.

Great Zimbabwe Ruins

The next day, on our way to Bulawayo, we stopped for lunch at Sir Garfield Todd's ranch, the father of my friend, Judy, and the Prime Minister of Rhodesia from 1953 to 1958. Judy joined us there. He and his wife were great hosts and arranged for us to tour the immense ranch in Land Rovers. Over lunch, we listened in rapt attention to their take on the roiling political situation under Ian Smith and his looming threat to unilaterally declare independence from Great Britain. While we were eating lunch, hippos were gamboling in the river below us.

Our next stop was the attractive City of Bulawayo, the largest urban center in southern Rhodesia. It is a spacious city with wide, attractive boulevards. We again had a special connection. Barbara and I had become friends in Washington with Saone Baron Crocker from Bulawayo, a graduate student at the Hopkins School of Advanced International Studies, and when she learned we were coming to her hometown, she arranged to be there to greet us. Her father, Ben Baron, was a well know solicitor and one of the leaders of the large Jewish community. Ben and his wife, Rachel, invited the entire group for cocktails at their large, imposing residence. It was there that I met, for the first time, a man I would come to cherish: Saone's brother, Marshall, who was also a solicitor, an artist, and a music critic. We would later become great friends in Washington. The entire family strongly supported enfranchising all underrepresented groups and actively opposed Ian Smith. Saone's husband, Chet Crocker, later became Assistant Secretary of State for African Affairs and then a professor at Georgetown University.

Our last activity in Bulawayo was a lecture by Dr. Hugh Ashton, author of the book "Problem Territories of Southern Africa" and a noted expert on the British protectorates, Basutoland, Bechuanaland, and Swaziland. We next took off from Bulawayo, headed toward Victoria Falls. We stopped at the Wankie Game Preserve on the way and, to my great delight, encountered elephants, kudus, impalas, giraffes, zebras, bushbucks and sable antelopes. We arrived at Victoria Falls the next morning in time for me to stroll through the muddy rain forest created by the mist from the falls. I then took the steep descent down to the "boiling point," a famous feature of the Zambesi River below the falls with its violently swirling eddies.

The famous Victoria Falls Hotel was itself an anachronism and a startling symbol of colonial confidence and chutzpah. It was immense. It still required gentlemen to appear for any of its meals in the dining room in coat and tie. It was almost comically

ENGLISH. I called it the Raj on the Zambesi. In residence at that time was a most remarkable specimen of humanity a great white hunter. The great white hunter was tall, ruggedly handsome, built like a professional wrestler and aggressively masculine. The ladies loved him. I was repelled by him since he was the epitome of manhood I'd spent my entire life up to that point avoiding. One of the memorable parts of our trip so far occurred when we took a motor launch tour of the Zambesi River above the falls (Marvin wondering what would happen should the launch lose power and we made a spectacular plunge 250 feet into the gorge). Highlights of the cruise included seeing some of the same animals we saw at Wankie, as well as crocodiles, goliath herons, whistling teals, and fish-eating eagles. The goliath heron was especially amazing with its seven-foot wingspan. To launch itself into the air, it has to run across the shallow water for a long distance before becoming airborne.

Goliath Heron Taking Flight

The elephants on one of the islands were grazing so close to us that we could almost touch them.

The next leg of the trip involved a flight from Livingston, Northern Rhodesia (soon to be independent Zambia) to Lusaka, the capital. We were met by Father Quinn, the principal of the Oppenheimer College of Social Services, who housed us in its dormitory. After a day of lectures and conferences with our consular officials, we hosted a reception attended by Dr. Kenneth Kaunda, the newly elected President. He and I had an interesting conversation, and I promised I would try to make it back to Lusaka later in the year for Zambia's independence celebration. Early the next morning, Dr. Randall, Marla Bush, Fred Njenga, and I had an appointment to visit with Dr. Kaunda in his office. I interviewed him with the fancy tape recorder I'd brought along. I concluded that he was one of the most impressive leaders we'd met so far, and I was optimistic about the country's prospects after independence.

The following day, we flew in a small plane to Ndola, the center of Zambia's famous copper mining industry. We were guests of the Rhodesian Selection Trust, a major producer of copper, in order to take a tour of its Roan Antelope Copper Mine. We were outfitted in white uniforms, boots, helmets and lamps and descended 2,490 feet into the bowels of the earth. I could only imagine what it must be like to work under such conditions, always under the threat of catastrophe. I was glad to see clouds and sky when we exited. That afternoon, we took a series of flights to our next destination, Nairobi, Kenya, where we had a layover of several days before flying to Uganda.

I took advantage of our hiatus by renting a car and driving into the countryside to see the Great Rift Valley and its enormous herds of antelope, giraffes, and other exotic creatures. I was startled to be driving along and suddenly encountering this great valley a thousand feet below. It is one of the few places in the world where you can simultaneously see two immense snowcapped volcanic peaks straddling the equator the rugged and irregular 17,000 feet Mt. Kenya and its cousin in Tanzania, Mt. Kilimanjaro at 19,300 feet. It is an awesome sight. I've always loved the story of how Queen Victoria decided to gift Kilimanjaro to her grandson, the German Kaiser, for his birthday, which explains its location in the German colony at the time.

Following our restful stay in Nairobi, we flew to Kampala, Uganda. Our small F-27 plane took almost 40 minutes to fly over Lake Victoria, putting the lake's vast size into perspective. We were housed at Makerere, then one of the great African universities, where we were warmly welcomed and benefited from a series of unusually interesting lectures. Uganda became independent in 1962, and although it initially retained the British monarch as its head of state, it later declared itself a republic while remaining a member of the Commonwealth. It is interesting that the nation has two official languages, Swahili and English. Swahili tends to be the lingua franca of the more isolated areas in the south. The US Embassy staff was especially impressive and provided us with detailed briefings on the situation in that area of East Africa. Our final lecture at Makerere was by Professor Colin Leys, an Oxford graduate and the head of the newly created Department of Political Science at the university. He was the author of a seminal book, "Politics in Southern Rhodesia," published in 1959, which accurately predicted the current situation in that country. The last meeting was with Uganda's Foreign Minister.

We returned by air to Nairobi, where we benefited from having Fred Njenga as part of our travelling seminar. We spent an enjoyable couple of hours with his uncle, Paul Koinange, who was Minister of Pan-African affairs and a relative of Uhuru Kenyatta, who later became President of Kenya. That afternoon at an official reception at city hall, I was seated with Jomo Kenyatta's daughter. Later, I met with the acting ambassador to Kenya, Mr. Dembos, to outline my preliminary plans for independent travel after the seminar ended. He politely told me that, in light of the chaotic events across Africa, my plans were impractical, if not completely impossible. I considered his counsel but decided to follow my itinerary anyway.

Early the next morning, the group took its last flight together to Addis Ababa. After our arrival and checking into our hotel, I could not wait to stroll around the city. I went almost directly to St. George's Cathedral, the principal church of the Ethiopian Coptic Church. It was indeed very different from any church I'd ever seen before. Dan Collier and I rented a car and drove to the old imperial palace and Haile's private zoo. Our guide there took us to see the imperial stables with their coach and matched white horses used to draw it, as well as the Arabians he loved to ride. We also glimpsed his 1934 Rolls-Royce limousine, which we were told had less than 1,000 miles on it since it was used only several times a year. The evening was given over to a farewell reception thanking Dr. Randall and his wife for their incredible management of our trip. I was truly astounded after all these months at how well he had handled so many sensitive situations with great diplomacy and in good spirits. I am, to this day, very grateful for the benefit of their calm and effective shepherding of such a diverse group.

From now on, I was on my own. My plans were my own. The fundamental motivation for my travels was really quite simple. I wanted to see as much of the rest of Africa as possible. After all, that is what the Army was paying me to do. I knew that what I was about to undertake was a bit risky and would test my fortitude, and perhaps that of others as well. I was quite naïve in thinking that the State Department and its representatives in the countries I was planning on visiting would share my enthusiasm. Their caution was undoubtedly engendered by what was happening in the Congo with the ongoing aftermath of the execution of Patrice Lumumba and the uprising in the Katanga Province, all of which was pitched in light of Soviet involvement and the Cold War.

I flew back to Nairobi to begin my journey. I met Fred and his friend, Augusto Bastos, the famous Paraguayan author, for dinner and drinks and then bade him a fond farewell. Bastos was in Nairobi as the representative of the Angolan Revolutionary Army. One of the most celebrated writers in the Spanish language, the Spanish Government awarded him the Cervantes Prize. At the embassy, I sent a cable to the embassy in Bangui, Central African Republic, requesting permission to visit and transit to Chad. By the time I flew out, I'd had no response. My flight to Leopoldville, Congo, was through Entebbe, Uganda. Our plane was a rickety old DC-6. In Entebbe, a group of Chinese officials boarded the plane on their way to Burundi, where they were working to destabilize parts of the eastern Congo. The Chinese delegation was quiet and impassive. I took out my notebook and started writing about them. They promptly did the same. When we landed in Bujumbura, Burundi, another group of Chinese officials was there to greet us.

I began to realize that Africa had become a mecca for the bizarre, the strange and the great unwashed of many countries. One should never have been surprised by what one was to encounter. At the airport in Bujumbura, I met an American orthodontist and his wife, who, for some reason, were unable to explain their presence in such a remote place. The other exotic creature I met there was an American woman appropriately named Mrs. Savage, who, it turns out, was pursuing her husband all over Africa. She had been scheduled to meet him at various rendezvous points, and when she arrived, a mysterious telegram would be waiting for her, indicating a new location for their meeting. I quickly realized she was quite crackers and began silently thinking that Mr. Savage was a smart man for avoiding her. The next interminable flight on the way to Leopoldville was to Luluabourg, Congo.

The scene at the Luluabourg airport was unbelievable and difficult to describe. The terminal was filthy, and the toilets did not work. Soldiers with their trucks and ambulances were surrounding the airport. A deserted United Nations plane and a crashed jet fighter near the runway lent authenticity to this wild scene. Hundreds of desperate Africans, waving their plane tickets and their tea pots (why tea pots?), were struggling with the military to board the next DC-6 to Leopoldville. Fortunately, with the aid of the military, transit passengers were allowed to board first.

Seated next to me were two young Africans in T-shirts and no shoes. They had obviously never flown before and were quite terrified. This was evident in their frantic grip on the seat in front of them during takeoff. Once in the air, one chap got a newspaper and was intently reading it while holding the paper upside down. The scene at the Leopold Airport was equally chaotic. As was the norm in much of Africa at the time, "dash" was everywhere. Dash was the term used to define the practice of scalping the innocent by demanding money from them for the most mundane practices, such as entering a country. At customs, they were attempting to tax my recorder and my camera. I then put on one of my most beautifully histrionic performances. Speaking in French, I brandished my official maroon passport, told them that I was a personal friend of the President of the Congo and that if I asked, he would come to rescue me if I was not admitted post haste. It worked.

Sabena was to have made reservations for me at the Memling Hotel. When I arrived there, they had never heard of me, and the hotel was completely full, as were all other hotels in the city mostly jammed with mercenaries from around the world. On the way back to the airport, I was mobbed by taxi drivers, shouting and pulling me in different directions. Once on board the bus, I ordered the driver to take me to the US Embassy. At the embassy,

I met Major Kohlbrand, who took me to his home for an overnight stay. I was exhausted.

The embassy folks decided that if I were to travel to Bangui, my best bet was to cross the Congo River to Brazzaville, where I could get a UTA Airlines connection. They also indicated that it would be hazardous to cross the river and that the situation in Brazzaville, the capital of French Congo, was in a tizzy in anticipation of a possible coup. The site where we were to take the launch across the river was filled with a long line of Africans who appeared to be refugees. I was given priority on the boat when, suddenly, out of nowhere, four Americans who were clearly military showed up. Off we went. The sheer size, volume and swiftness of the Congo took my breath away. When we arrived at the port in Brazzaville, I asked the four Americans if they spoke French. None did so I had to translate for them and facilitate their way through customs. I later found out they were pilots who'd been flying clandestine missions in the Congo.

Since I had flight reservations at the airport, I went there directly only to find out my flight had been delayed by an unbelievable 9 hours. I met several American embassy staffers there who took a message from me to Col. Ross Franklin, the Army attaché, whom I'd met before. He and a warrant officer came to the airport and took me in their car. I was then illegally in the country since I was on a transit visa and had no business staying there for any length of time. To make matters even more dramatic, Col. Franklin took me to the office of the Deputy Foreign Minister, where he was negotiating the return of our Air Attaché in Bangui and the release of a NASA C-130 which had been impounded. He then told me that I was not welcome in the Central African Republic. He called the ambassador there, who relented and let me stay in transit status. I had lunch at the Franklins' quarters and swam in their pool before returning to the airport.

On arrival in Bangui, I was met at the airport by Ambassador George Ross and his principal staff. It was a warm welcome personally, but a guarded one officially. They registered me at the Rock Hotel, where I went to bed, confused, tired, and slightly disgusted with my unknown destiny. Just before crawling into bed, I looked out my window and below me was what appeared to be a great valley. Imagine my surprise the next morning when I went to the window again, only to discover that the dark valley was, in reality, the majestic Ubangi River, a major tributary of the Congo. At a mid-morning meeting with the ambassador and his staff, for reasons unclear to me, I was informed that Mr. Moss must leave Bangui toute suite. They'd talked to the embassy in Fort Lamy, Chad, where I was welcome to stay for several days. Ambassador and Mrs. Ross kindly invited me to swim in their pool and to dinner at the residence.

The next day, the embassy driver hustled me to the airport for my flight to Chad. I was met at the airport by Ambassador Brewster Morris and his wife. After greetings, I was driven to my hotel, which looked like a prop from a bad French Foreign Legion B-grade film. Unfortunately, it was the only hotel open in the city at the time. After a rudimentary breakfast at my bleak hotel, I went immediately to the impressive Chari River, an 800-mile-long river that flows into Lake Chad and thus never reaches the sea.

People were bathing, fishing, washing clothes, loading barges, building dugouts and praying a wonderful and delightful scene of human activity. The fish most often caught in the river is the Nile perch, which is one of the world's largest freshwater fish obtaining a length of over 6 feet and weighing up to 200 pounds.

That evening, the deputy chief of mission, Mike Smith, picked me up and drove me to the ambassador's residence for dinner and bridge. Ambassador Morris and his wife were warm hosts. They had adopted a duiker (also called a dik-dik), the smallest of all antelopes, which was a delight with its dainty hoofs the size of fingernails and its enormous eyes.

Two nights later, they had a cocktail party which included the French ambassador and some of his staff. At that point, I really began to realize that the life of a US ambassador in such a country is a relatively lonely existence, which is probably why I was wined and dined for much of the time I was there. I was also wondering why we had an embassy there at all.

I'd decided I wanted to see more of West Africa, so I made plans to fly from Ft Lamy to Doula, Cameroon. Our plane made a bumpy landing on what appeared to be a dirt runway for a one-hour layover in the unusual city of Ngaoundere, in Northern Cameroon. It lies in a bowl surrounded by low, beautifully vegetated mountains on a high plateau. The city was part of the German colony until after World War II, when it became a French protectorate. We arrived safely in Doula in the late morning. Douala is Cameroon's largest city and its major port. It is also one of the rainiest cities in the world, as the next few days dramatically illustrated. It also has the distinction of being within sight of one of Africa's highest and most active volcanoes, the 13,000-foot-high Mt. Cameroon, which is covered by rain forest and is seldom visible from below due to the intensely foggy wet climate. I never even got a glimpse of it. Not too far from the mountain is Lake Nyos, a volcanic caldera where a landslide in 1986 caused a massive eruption of carbon dioxide from the lake, killing almost 1,500 people in the surrounding villages and an equal number of cattle. It was the largest such carbon dioxide asphyxiation known in modern times.

I took a taxi to the consulate to announce my presence. The embassy in Ft Lamy had cabled them about me, but when I arrived, they had no clue who I was or why I was there. I checked into the rather nice Hotel des Cocotiers and returned to the consulate to meet with Andy Antipas, the acting consul general, who gave me an outstanding briefing on Cameroon, followed by a tour of the city. That evening, at the suggestion of several junior staff members at the consulate, we went to an African nightclub, where I was fascinated by the band playing a fusion of rock and roll with indigenous music, all involving the use of local xylophone-like instruments and large drums. The music was hypnotic.

My next stop before heading back to Rhodesia was Libreville, Gabon, where I stayed at the pleasant Hotel du Roi Denis near the beach. Libreville is the capital as well as the largest city in the country. Dick Divine, the vice-consul general, hosted me, gave me a detailed summary of current happenings in the country, and had drinks and dinner with me at his residence. He helped me make arrangements to fly to Salisbury, which I did via Pointe Noire, Congo, and Brazzaville, where I was once again hosted by Col. Franklin. The flight from Gabon to Brazzaville was terrifying. I was the only passenger, and after takeoff, I heard loud banging coming from behind a curtain at the rear of the passenger compartment. I asked the steward what it was. He opened the curtain, and there I saw dozens of beef carcasses hanging from hooks, banging against the side of the plane. That and turbulence caused me to drink every libation available enroute. Thus, my independent travel, an odyssey marked by uncertainty, difficulties and tribulations, ended. Did I learn more about the countries and regions I'd traveled through? The answer is a very positive yes. I had also been the recipient of untold kindnesses from a host of people I will never forget.

Chapter 8
Rhodesia – Fall of 1964

In late summer, I flew back to Salisbury to begin what turned out to be one of the great adventures of my life five months of study at the University College of Rhodesia and Nyasaland, which we had visited earlier in our trip. I was excited about the prospect, since I'd been impressed by the facilities, faculty, and students during my previous stay there. One other officer in the group, Al Steffen, was to be there as well. Although we were not there for a specific purpose other than learning more about Africa, I decided that my goal was to complete the research for and write my master's thesis on a subject of my choosing. I checked in with the US Consulate, which was in the center of the city, so they knew I was staying in the country for up to 5 months, which also gave me access to its commissary, stocked with my favorite liquor brands.

Another aspect that excited me was that the university was a major social and political experiment by bringing together the principal ethnic groups of the country African, European, Colored, and Asian for the first time in a single higher education institution. I realized that the tensions in Rhodesia, so rife then, probably made this experiment difficult to carry out, and one of the things I wanted to learn was how successful it was.

I was assigned a young tutor who was curious about why a US Army officer was studying at his university. I explained that the Army was doing so to have officers become experts in various parts of the world, ensuring we had competent advisors on hand when needed. When queried about what I intended to do while in residence, I outlined my thoughts on my thesis subject, which had been triggered by what I'd been reading since arriving there. It was a period of great chaos in Rhodesia, with a Prime Minister, Ian Smith, who was clamping down on freedom of speech and threatening to close down media outlets written for or popular with African and other non-white audiences. Right before I arrived, Smith had forced the one and only weekly African newspaper, The African Daily News, to cease publication. My subject was to be a critical analysis of press-government relations in the country in the current political setting. His reaction was immediate and negative, stating rather boldly that my subject was too controversial and that I should select something else. Although he did not say it, I assumed he was thinking it could have a negative effect on the university and its experiment in multiracial education. I did not see how that would happen, and I elected to ignore his advice.

As a result of the forced closure of the African Daily News, the only widely circulated African newspaper in the country, a multiracial group of about 75 students protested before parliament and government house against the Smith government's actions. They were all arrested and arraigned, and when I arrived were awaiting trial. This was, of course, one of the motivations for my thesis. I wanted to research and write about the advent of the British journalistic tradition across all of southern Africa, including Rhodesia, and the recent attempts to undermine and defy that tradition. The actual title of my thesis was "A Critical Analysis of the Rhodesian Press and Its Role in Contemporary Rhodesian Politics and Society."

Early on at the university, I renewed my friendship with Judy Todd and met her best friend and fellow student, Hillary Cookson. Both had been arrested. They frequently invited me to their rooms after dinner to discuss this and other events in Rhodesia. They were both extraordinarily beautiful, highly intelligent and fascinated by having an American officer sympathetic to their causes. They told me that Lord and Lady Richard Acton were paying for the defense in their pending trial. Lord Acton had the wonderful title, at least to American ears, of John Lyon-Dalberg Acton, 3rd Baron Acton. He was one of the few Catholic hereditary peers in the House of Lords, and they had 11 children. They lived on a large, impressive estate and horse farm some miles away from Salisbury. Judy introduced me to them by relating my thesis subject, which was of great interest to them. Among his other notable accomplishments, he had founded the National Club in Salisbury, the first major social club open to all races.

Once I'd met the Actons, they began inviting me to join them at the Saturday races at Salisbury's very traditional half-mile track, where they raced many of their thoroughbreds. They had a box at the track. The second time I joined them there, they introduced me to their guests. The guests were the Duke and Duchess of Montrose, who held even more amazing titles, including the 8th Duke of Montrose, Premier Duke of Scotland,

Earl of Kincardine, and Marquess Graham. In the face of such daunting titles, I was introduced as Captain Marvin Moss, US Army, a bit shorter moniker. We got along famously.

I set out to outline in my mind what I proposed to do for my thesis, realizing that I had only 4 months to conduct the research and to write it. I managed to get introductions to several of the editors of major papers, including the most important one, the Rhodesia Herald, the single largest daily paper by circulation in the country and owned by a South African media company. That company's history and the Herald's early days clearly indicated that the storied tradition of English journalism was the prevailing one here. By that tradition, I mean a style of reporting featuring fact-based stories with controversial or analytical content limited to the editorial page, and a permanent staff trained in that style. I was also conducting research at the national and university libraries, reading 10 years of newspapers and taking detailed notes on their content.

It became obvious to me that, in the minds of the students, I was already aligned with the majority, those opposed to Ian Smith and the Rhodesia Front, the ruling party. This identification was fostered by my association with Judy and her friends and Byron Hove. I'd also become friends with an interesting cross-section of other students. An amusing event happened as a result of that. The Student Union had called a special meeting of all students to consider a resolution condemning the closing of the African Daily News and opposing any unilateral declaration of independence. The vocal minority of Smith supporters, all White, was, of course, there but badly outnumbered. I was sitting in the audience when one of them asked for recognition and requested that I be either removed from the meeting or prevented from voting. Byron called on me to respond. I said that although I was an American citizen and an officer in its armed forces, I was a legitimately registered student and, under the rules of the Union, eligible to vote. My speech brought loud cheers and a prolonged ovation, followed immediately by my supporters sitting behind me rising and singing very badly the first lines of the Star-Spangled Banner. I was deeply moved.

My student fans (mostly the previously mentioned three stooges) decided to test my mettle through a series of pranks. The first was one morning when I woke up to find they had removed the knob from my door and wedged it shut. I very badly needed to go to the bathroom and could not get out (there was also no telephone in my room). I knew there was a wide ledge outside my window that might give me access to the bathroom, so I went out my window and was carefully walking along (I was on the second floor) when I heard a loud voice crying out, "Captain Moss, what on earth are you doing?" It was none other than Sir Charles Cummings, the university principal. I explained my predicament, and he sent a locksmith to my rescue. A week or so later, I was out drinking into the wee hours with Judy and friends when I came back to my quarters. I opened the door and reached in to switch on the light as I usually did. There was a loud explosion in the room. The stooges had cracked the overhead light bulb, attached a cherry bomb to it, and covered it with a bag of flour, which now coated everything in the room, including all my 3x5 cards strewn about in preparation for organizing my thesis. In my bed was a complete, real human skeleton with a pipe in its mouth, cherries for eyes, and a top hat. Fastened to the window was the following large sign: "The American Fighting Man is Always Vigilant." Needless to say, Sir Charles was there in a thrice and bemoaned my presence at the university. I politely pointed out to him that I hadn't caused the chaos, but his beloved students had perpetrated the pranks.

One university student I'd grown close to was a tall, handsome man named Leggy Linnell (I never did know his real first name). His family owned one of the largest tobacco farms in the country, and he invited me to spend a weekend there. I'd become fascinated by the ancient cave paintings I'd seen when some of the African students took me 30 miles north of Salisbury to the Domboshawa Rocks, a massive rock outcropping with many caves and paintings dating back as far as 6,000 years.

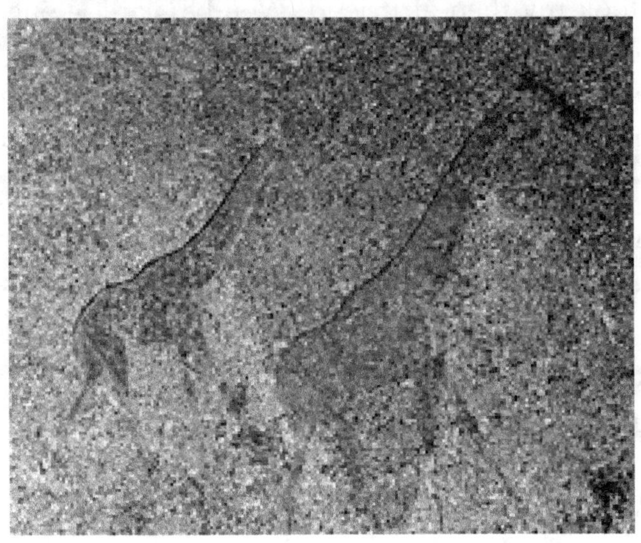

Zimbabwe Cave Painting

Leggy led me on a series of hikes to the kopjes (the Afrikaans word for the ubiquitous rock formations) on his farm. I photographed many of them; however, those photos have not survived. It was an interesting weekend. His parents were great hosts. The farm was, in many ways, a self-contained universe with its swimming pool, squash court, and other amenities. Their African workers were well housed and seemed to be happy there.

As I was expanding my outreach and conducting research in archives of previous newspaper articles, it was announced that the High Court had exonerated all the student demonstrators due to a lack of clear evidence, caused by the ineptitude of the arresting officers. Most of the campus was jubilant. The Actons then invited all of the indicted students and me to their mansion for a victory celebration. It very quickly became my promotion party in Germany redux. They had an open bar and a buffet dinner. I took my then-girlfriend, Wendy Clark, along. I was in the immense dining room when I saw that some of the African students, unused as they were to an open bar, had become quite drunk. I'll never forget one of the young Acton daughters rushing to the side of her mother, Lady Acton, and yelling "Mummy, another African has fallen off the balcony." Under the enormous dining room table was an Aubusson carpet at least 40 feet long and probably dating back to the 18th Century. I felt a tug at my leg, and there was young Lord Richard Acton under the table, brandishing a silent butler picking up the lighted cigarette butts from the carpet. As I was preparing to leave, I could not find Wendy. As I headed for the car, I heard moaning from the rose garden. Wendy, also quite intoxicated, had walked over a brick wall and fallen into the rose bushes. I extracted her and placed her delicately in the car.

Knowing that Zambia was about to celebrate its independence in early October, I invited Wendy Clark to join me at that event. Two days before the celebration on October 4th, we drove to Lusaka. I was trying to figure out how we could get a ringside seat. I once again did something that could have easily gotten me cast out of the Army I registered as a reporter for the Baltimore Sun, with Wendy as my photographer. The Sun at that time had a large and respected foreign bureau, but I figured they would not be there for this event. Fortunately, I was correct. The event was magical. We were seated in the press box and allowed to roam freely on the stadium field, the site of the celebration. It started with a massive festival, with thousands of men and women from different tribes across the country dancing to their own music as the sun set. President Kaunda arrived in his new car, a garish Chrysler convertible given to him by the United States, with copper bumpers. We watched as he and Princess Alice, the Princess Royal, as she was called, the Queen's aunt and the last surviving granddaughter of Queen Victoria, lowered the Union Jack at midnight and raised the flag of Zambia. Memorable.

By the middle of December, I'd organized my thesis and finished writing most of it. In the end, it turned out to be more than an analysis of press-government relations, and rereading it recently, I realized it was also a cogent history of the country's politics leading to the inevitable climax of the Unilateral Declaration of Independence in November 1965. Nearing the end of my studies, I organized a large farewell party at a local social club and invited the entire university, many of whom attended. I served bourbon to many of them for the first time. It was a dramatic end to my short stay. As I was boarding my plane at the Salisbury Airport, many of my loyal devotees were on the observation deck to see me off. There was also a family of American missionaries boarding the same plane with me. Suddenly, I heard loud yelling and looked back as did the missionaries. The Three Stooges and the others had unfurled a large banner saying, "Yankee, Go Home," to the astonishment of my fellow travelers.

Why has this Rhodesia interlude remained such an important part of my life for these many years? I believe the answer is that I made many friends in a short period of time, researched and wrote an important document on Rhodesian history, and experienced a university system that operated very differently from ours. By that I mean the university college had essentially the English system in Africa whereby the students are very independent, can attend lectures on any subjects or not, can live it up and elect to study or not, but in the end have to pass a series of serious, rigorous and difficult exams graded both in Salisbury and in London. I came to admire that system because it seemed to require a level of maturity and sophistication absent in American academia. And finally, I found the students to be much more sexually liberated than I'd found anywhere else including acceptance of gay folks. In short, I grew up there. I must have made a lasting impression. Many years later, my friends, Joe and Bettye Pegues, were sent to open a Morgan Bank subsidiary in Rhodesia. They held a cocktail party and invited a who's who of the country, including Judy Todd. When asked if she knew Marvin Moss, her reply was, "Who could forget Marvin?"

I had now traveled and studied in much of sub-Saharan Africa for almost 7 months. The African people, in all their diverse manifestations, intrigued me, and I now felt a bond with them as they were ditching their colonial pasts and struggling under less-than-ideal conditions to establish new governments and institutions. I was probably more than a bit naïve in thinking that this transition would be an orderly one, resulting in economic and political stability in many of the newly independent nations.

Looking back on my travels and studies in Africa in 1964, I would be remiss if I did not discuss the rather overwhelming context in which US relations with the continent were viewed. It was a period of great alarm over the extension of Soviet influence throughout the Middle East and Africa, especially following Nasser's coup in Egypt and his leadership in urging non-alignment among many countries in the region. The tragic story of the Belgian Congo in the early 1960's added even more fuel to the fire. During my stint in the Pentagon as a briefer for the Joint Chiefs on Africa, I was astounded at their overreaction and that of the intelligence community to the slightest incursions in Africa. I cite the provision of a few tanks to Ghana and Algeria as an example. I knew full well that these modern weapons would, within a few months or years, be rusting and useless somewhere in both countries. Nonetheless, we were expected to treat these Soviet actions as if they were apocalyptic and major Cold War challenges. They were, of course, simply irrelevant in the long run.

Now, there are great examples such as Kenya and Ghana of relatively stable and vibrant countries; however, many continue to struggle. In retrospect, the post-independence success or failure of many of these countries is, I believe, directly attributable to their colonial experience. Especially egregious, of course, is the former Belgian Congo, which had been ruled as the personal fiefdom of King Leopold of Belgium. However, that generality is belied by countries such as Uganda, which had a fairly enlightened colonial experience but has subsequently become tragically anarchic. The fact that I subsequently sought to return to my next assignment in Africa is an indication of the feelings I had for the continent and its people.

When I left Washington on this epic sojourn, my political leanings were trending to be supportive of Democratic candidates at the state and national levels. My trip through Africa convinced me of the importance of having a government in Washington that recognized it could play a pivotal role in assisting these new nations, and that the Democratic Party was most likely to do so.

My family was scattered throughout the world at the time. I was in Africa. Phil had gone off to study at the University of Nancy in eastern France, and my mother and my great Aunt Barbara were on a cruise in the Mediterranean. To meet them, Phil rode his Vespa over the Alps and joined them in Nice. During the cruise, Mom evidently had an affair with a Jewish man from Brooklyn, and Aunt Barbara (my Auntie Mame) became the favorite of some crew members, so she disappeared down into the crew quarters for days at a time, drinking and entertaining her aficionados. When the ship docked in New York, my mom's beau was met by his up to that time secret wife.

Chapter 9
Ethiopia 1965-1966

When asked by my career officer in the Pentagon about my next assignment, I indicated that my experience in Africa led me to want to be stationed at Kagnew Station in Asmara, Ethiopia (now Eritrea), to be back on the continent. He agreed with me and facilitated my assignment. President Johnson had just been re-elected in November 1964, and I managed to be invited to one of his inaugural balls. I invited my friend, Irma Ireland, to be my guest. I was wearing my rented tux, and she, despite her athletic interests and indifference to most feminine guiles, was sporting a ball gown. We were seated with a rich mix of highly inebriated and, to my mind, typically wealthy Texans.

Knowing my mother well, I assumed at some stage she would remarry. It happened faster than I'd anticipated when she became engaged to Ira Roth, whom I'd known tangentially through our Lutheran church. He was frequently the smiling greeter passing out the Sunday bulletin. He was very different from Mom (and me) in many ways, having been raised in a Pennsylvania Dutch manner in Pennsylvania. They were married in March 1965 at our church, Trinity Lutheran in Hagerstown, followed by a reception at a local restaurant. I was part of the wedding party. Ira's daughter, Jean, who lived in Hagerstown and his son, Bill, were also in the wedding party, so Phil and I acquired a step-sister and step-brother. Phil was not there because he was in France, where he eventually met his American wife, Jean. I think all of them, from the very beginning, found me a bit much to take.

My orders were that I should arrive in Asmara, Ethiopia, at the end of March 1965. As always, I decided that my journey there would be a typically convoluted one. I asked Phil to meet me in Paris and, from there, visit Nancy. And then on a skiing trip to the places I knew best in Germany. On the first night in Paris, I bought tickets to the Opéra National de Paris, affectionately known to Parisians as the Palais Garnier after its architect. It is indeed a palace. On offer that evening was an obscure opera by the 18th-century composer, Jean-Philippe Rameau, entitled "Les Indes Galantes," which I had never heard of before. It turned out to be, quite by accident, the funniest evening in an opera house I'd ever spent. It is an opera-ballet about love in four exotic locales the Ottoman Empire, Peru, Persia and North America. It made no sense to either of us, although both of us then spoke fairly decent French.

Toward the end of Act One there was a battle scene. Huge cannons were hauled on the stage and fired. Immense clouds of smoke immediately enveloped the stage, the singing stopped, the miasma rolled through the proscenium arch into the orchestra, which stopped playing and kept going through the first rows of seats. Phil and I were laughing hysterically while the French around us remained stoically quiet. Then le Directeur General de l'Opéra National de Paris (one has to say this quickly with a French accent to get the full humor of it all) in his beautifully tailored Pierre Cardin suit came out to announce that there had been "une faute." I thought that was already obvious. The second act was equally funny. Children, dressed as tiny cupids sporting bows and arrows, started descending from the sky, accompanied by the great creaking and groaning of the machinery that made their descent possible. At that point, with a loud bang, the whole process ceased, leaving the frightened children suspended 60 feet above the stage. Once again, the great curtain came down, and the ever-elegant Monsieur le Directeur General de l'Opéra National de Paris (try it again in French and see if you can keep a straight face) came thither to announce encore une faute. By this time, I was practically on the floor laughing to the point that les Francais nearby were highly incensed at the Americans' crude behavior. I decided that we'd blundered into the Opera Comique by mistake. We thoroughly enjoyed the evening despite the fact that we were the only ones rooting throughout for les indes galantes. It was the most remarkable evening at the opera since my genitals were assaulted by the dwarf during Aida at the Met.

From Paris, we drove in a rental VW with a ski rack to see Phil's lodging at the university in Nancy. He had an apartment that was rather elegant for a student. He was enjoying his studies and meeting the wonderful mix of students, including a fair number of non-French speakers. I'd brought my old wooden skis with me. From there, we drove to one of my old skiing haunts in Bavaria, Oberstdorf Nebelhorn, a small village in a valley surrounded by the Austrian Alps. I always preferred it because it was small and quaint, and the skiing was very easy. We checked into a small gasthaus for several days and skied almost all the mountains by the time we left. I dropped Phil off in Nancy and drove back to Paris, where I managed to snag a ticket for Maria Callas' last performance of Tosca again at the Palais Garnier. By that time, her voice was really gone, but her acting was superb, especially during the murder of Scarpia and at the end, as she hurled herself off the ramparts of Castel Sant'Angelo.

I had no idea what to expect with my assignment at Kagnew Station, but I surmised that there would be some anticipation of my arrival, given that I was a paratrooper and West Point graduate with a degree in international relations. You must remember that I still looked at least 10 years younger than my age, and in the states was constantly being carded in bars. The flight to Asmara was from Athens. Due to our agreement with Ethiopia, you had to arrive and depart the country in civilian attire. We landed, and I grabbed my skis and my hand luggage and was coming down the ramp with my skis over my shoulders when I was greeted by an officer who asked me, "Young man, we are expecting a Captain Moss on this flight. Have you seen him?" You can imagine the reaction when I, with my skis, announced that I was the genuine article. The entire greeting party's faces fell. I was loaded into the staff car and stared at as if I were a Martian.

Kagnew Station, located almost in the center of Asmara, was a major communications facility involving the Army, Navy and various intelligence agencies. It was located there due to its location and altitude. Asmara was almost 8,000 feet above sea level, thus providing it with the capability to communicate with major commands at sea and in Europe, and to listen in on signals from as far away as the Soviet Union. The post was attractive and had everything Americans abroad insisted upon, including school, hospital, PX, commissary, bowling alley, churches, quarters, and other amenities. It was carefully protected by walls and wire from the local citizens. The climate was unbelievably salubrious, with daily temperatures in the mid-70's year-round and little rain until the fall, when precipitation was plentiful for 3 or 4 months.

The city had existed prior to the Italian invasion in the late 19th Century, but after the occupation, it grew considerably and began to reflect Italy's cityscapes and architecture. The modernist idiom became fully developed after Mussolini's 1935 invasion, and the entire city has now been designated a World Heritage Site for its unique collection of modernist architecture. Visiting some of its streets and palm-fringed boulevards, you can imagine being in a town in Calabria. One of its most iconic buildings is the Fiat Tagliero gas station, pictured below.

Italian had also become the lingua franca in light of the daunting number of local languages. The population included a group, which we and Italians called "the café lattes." They were the product of the early colonial years, when there were few Italian women. The women and the men were quite striking, having the best features of the locals and their Italian occupiers.

My first assignment was to be the troop commander for all the soldiers stationed there with the Army's Strategic Communications Command - some 250 troops in all. The previous commander had been a bit lax in his command. The city was under a 9 pm curfew due to recent rumblings of an anti-Ethiopian insurrection and several violent incidents. My predecessor was not enforcing it, and when he did, he was meting out minimum punishments. I decided, despite my juvenile appearance, to crack down smartly, which I did. My first sergeant was delighted when some of the troops took my command photo in the hallway and smashed it. Sgt. Meade told me it was a sign I was making progress.

I was initially living in the BOQ on post, in a dingy one-room unit with a bathroom. I disliked it intensely and began scouting for an Italian apartment in the city. I found one in a wonderful location. It was directly opposite Haile Selassie's Asmara palace, which housed a private zoo. I would wake up in the morning to the roar of his lions. I later met his tennis pro and played on the imperial court. The apartment was spacious, with a living room, two bedrooms, a kitchen, and a bath.

There was to be a post-wide tennis tournament, and, in desperation to fill out the Army team, some of my junior officers recruited me to join, although they had no idea of my competence.

I drew as my first opponent a young Navy Lt. who had been captain of the University of Pennsylvania tennis team. He was to serve first. I decided I was going to make a brave show at the beginning of the match. He slammed a perfect serve to me. I hit it back with great force down the line opposite his serving side and won a triumphant first point. It was the last one in the entire match.

Once again, I was shocked by the insularity of the officers and enlisted on the post. They infrequently ventured forth into the city (except to visit the bars with beautiful café-latte women), learned no Italian, and ignored the rich culture of the Ethiopian people surrounding them. I began taking Italian lessons almost as soon as I moved to my apartment. My teacher was an attractive middle-aged woman who was a superb teacher, and I picked it up quickly. * I was also renting a Land Rover and a driver to take me and one of my lieutenants, David Dethero, to places important in the country's history, including its old imperial capital, Axum.

*An interesting footnote to my Italian instruction. In preparation for a long trip to Italy a few years ago, I decided to hire an instructor at Speak in Charlottesville to hone my ability. In the very first interview, she asked me in Italian where I learned the language, and I responded in Italian. She immediately began to laugh. I asked her why. She responded: "You are speaking 19th-century Italian. The language has changed remarkably since then." I realized then that the language I learned was the one brought to Asmara in 1892.

David and I became good friends, and I proposed a long trip to southern Africa that I would organize and lead. He agreed, although as a rather diffident person, he was a bit hesitant. At any rate, off we went in November 1965, flying first to Nairobi. We stayed at Tree Tops, a beautiful hotel in the mountains overlooking a water hole where Princess Elizabeth was when her father died. They met you at your bus and, with a rifleman accompanying you, took you through the bush to the pull-down ladder that leads to the elevated hotel. Once safely inside, the ladder is pulled up, and there you are. Despite its rustic appearance, it is rather elegant. We had our own room. I left the window in the room open when we went to the roof deck for cocktails. I'd forgotten to take my camera and went back to the room to fetch it. When I entered the room, a baboon had come through the window, picked up my camera and slung it over its shoulder as if it were a professional photographer. I yelled loudly. It dropped the camera and fled. That evening, we watched, by moonlight, many elephants, antelopes, and other beasts feeding at the water hole.

We then flew to Lusaka to visit my old friend from the university, Wendy Clark and her new husband. It was a warm reunion with one of my favorite friends from Salisbury and then on to Victoria Falls. I again arranged for David to do the same things we'd done the previous year. We also chartered a small plane and flew west into Namibia's Caprivi Strip to view the immense herds of elephants and antelopes. I loved it. David got airsick. It was now November 11, 1965. After touring the falls and the rain forest, we returned to the hotel and went to the bar for a drink. The bartender was ecstatic. Ian Smith had just declared his Unilateral Declaration of Independence from Great Britain (UDI), and the bartender was an enthusiastic RF supporter. I grabbed my drink and fled in lieu of getting into an argument. I was very despondent that this had finally happened, although I'd known for some time that it was inevitable.

We took the overnight train the next day to Bulawayo, where we were to stay with the Barons. David was panicked on the train trip, thinking that revolutionaries were going to throw bombs through our compartment window. Marshall Baron met us at the station and took us to the Baron's lovely home. He took the two of us up to his room, dressed in his yellow bikini, put on the haunting adagietto of Mahler's 5th Symphony (almost a gay anthem) and proceeded to do his yoga by standing on his head for 30 minutes. David was, of course, nonplussed and did not know what to say. I merely chuckled.

The Barons, being strongly opposed to Smith and UDI, were in a state of shock and brooding sorrow. They, however, were hosting us for a festive dinner, so we started with our cocktails. Marshall had told me that a special guest was coming to join us for dinner. I queried him about the guest. He finally told us that she was one of the world's most renowned experts on Marcel Proust. She arrived. A diminutive woman toting a high-powered rifle as tall as she was, since she lived in the outback and had to go through lion-infested country to catch the bus. David and I were fascinated.

The next day, Marshall took us into a beautiful natural area, the Matopos Hills, where Cecil John Rhodes lived and is buried. His grave is at the highest point on the plateau and offers a glorious view of the rugged countryside. That evening after dinner, Ben Baron pulled me aside for a private conversation. It seems that not only had Smith declared UDI, but he had also placed a moratorium on the export of any currency from Rhodesia. His youngest daughter was then at university in South Africa, and he needed to get money out of the country to support her education. He asked me if I would take a significant amount of cash along with me when I went to South Africa. He was convinced that I could get away with it since I was traveling on an American official passport. Since I admired and respected the family so much, I reluctantly agreed to his proposition. I did not tell David what I was about to do lest he panic.

We flew to Salisbury, and I returned for a reunion of sorts at the university, although most of my friends there had been seniors and were gone. My friend, Hillary Cookson, had married young Lord Acton and thus became Baroness Acton. Judy Todd was in England. After a reunion with my remaining friends, we decided to move on to South Africa. We managed to get through customs with a heavy bag full of English pounds and Rhodesian currency. To this day, I have no idea how much money was in the bag. We were met at the airport by Ben's daughter, and I transferred the money to her. We flew on to Cape Town, which I found to be one of the most beautiful cities I'd ever seen. We did extensive local touring, including taking the cable car to the summit of Table Mountain and visiting one of South Africa's most famous vineyards, Groot Constantia. The house there is the best-preserved 17th-century Dutch dwelling in the country. The house, its vineyard, and the surrounding countryside are magnificent.

**Groot Constantia note the slight similarity to
Glen Burnie's Dutch Revival curvilinear gables**

We returned to Asmara after another epic journey.

Soon thereafter, I again rented a Land Rover and driver to head toward Mekele, the capital of Tigray Province, the area of the present tragic war. Enroute, David and I picked up two Peace Corps volunteers who were headed in the same direction. One was a tall, handsome Swedish-American from Wisconsin. In Mekele, we were staying in a strange hotel that looked very much like an ancient Greek fortress in the Peloponnese. It was owned and operated by a young Asian Indian couple. My group gathered on the hotel terrace for drinks when we noticed that there was a mule tethered in front. Soon, an ancient English lady joined us. Upon questioning, it became apparent that it was her mule, and the following tale ensued. She was the widow of one of the British commanding generals during the war against Italy in Abyssinia during World War II. She had his war diary and was dutifully following it around Ethiopia in tribute to him and his military exploits. All this was carried out on the mule. I've alluded before to the strange, exotic Europeans one meets in Africa, but this one took the prize.

Although I prided myself on knowing much about Ethiopia and its people, I'd not known that we had arrived in Mekele on the holiest day of Coptic Christianity Easter. We were invited in the evening for the commencement of services in the beautiful round church below the hotel. Congregants were led by priests through the narthex, hand bells and incense in hand. It was very moving. Meanwhile, the hills around the church and hotel were filling with thousands of worshipers. After sunset and the end of the liturgy, the women began ululating as they lit fires to roast their goats and lambs for the breaking of the fast and their festive meal. The hills were now a spectacular scene of celebration. It is seared in my memory.

Only later did I learn that there had been a tragic element to our trip. The very healthy, tall Peace Corps volunteer we'd brought along had gone on to visit friends near the Blue Nile. While swimming in the river, he was attacked and eaten by a giant Nile crocodile. His remains were evidently never found. We held a memorial service for him in the chapel at Kagnew Station with dozens of his grieving Peace Corps friends in attendance.

A few friends of mine at Kagnew Station were reaching out to the local community, including its small diplomatic community. Tony and Betty Vydra introduced me to the US consul general, Sam Gammon*, and his wife (Sam is still living at 98 and is a resident of Westminster Canterbury in Charlottesville, VA). They invited me to have dinner at their residence several times, and at one such gathering, I met Lord and Lady Bromley, the honorary consul general of Great Britain. The first time I had dinner at the Bromley residence, I was sitting at the table when suddenly my legs were violently pushed apart, and there staring at me was their pet cheetah, whose mouth was then only inches away from my crotch. They laughed and apologized for not warning me about their beloved pet. The Bromleys fit in nicely with my American concept of the eccentric English expatriate in Africa. My Italian was then sufficiently proficient that I was also playing bridge in that language at the Asmara Italian Club (Circolo Italiano).

*Years later, Sam was appointed ambassador by President Carter to the Indian Ocean island nation of Mauritius from 1978 to 1980. He resigned after two years by sending a now-legendary cable to the State Department, stating boldly that there was no strategic US interest, or, for that matter, any interest at all, in Mauritius, nor any reason to have an embassy there, and that he and his wife were coming home.

In early 1966, I was reassigned to command a small unit in a remote valley south of Asmara near the old Italian settlement of Decamare. We were given the responsibility for constructing and operating a new satellite communications system, which involved connecting the rig to newly launched satellites in synchronous orbit around the Earth. My first sergeant was the indispensable Sergeant Trapasso. He was a strapping macho man, whom the troops adored and respected highly. * One of the interesting features of our location was the WW II air strip which abutted our site. It was over a mile long and had been used to transship material from Europe to the Asian Front. It was still in excellent condition. Nearby was a Catholic orphanage for young Ethiopian girls run by a charming and tireless red-headed Italian nun. I adopted the orphanage and collected funds for its operation among the officers at Kagnew Station, and enlisted my mother as well, who was sending books and used clothing.

*Master Sergeant Trapasso wrote me this letter in December 1966 while he was still stationed in Asmara. It reads in part, "Dear Sir, This letter constitutes two firsts for me. It's the first time I have addressed an officer as "dear" and it's the first letter I've written in 10 years. …I've been sitting here trying to figure out how to say this without it sounding wrong, but to put it simply, we miss you very much. It seems the Transportable Division has lost much of its esprit. Some of the men are still coming out with 'When Captain Moss was here…' …My point, sir, is that the men haven't forgotten you. I have never seen an officer who was held in such high esteem by his men. Most of them would follow you to hell, and I'd be there to kick their asses into line."

In 1965, my mother, stepfather and Coffman's came for a visit. I organized a cocktail party to greet them at one of the early Italian villas overlooking Asmara. Our rather worthless commanding officer, Lt. Col Underwood Spivey (I always referred to him as Underwear Spivey), invited them for drinks at his quarters. He was known for his parsimony. After her first drink, my mother, who loved her cocktails, was not offered another. She very loudly shook the ice cubes in her drink until she received a refill. I was very proud of her. She went native and had a seamstress make her a traditional outfit.

I was also teaching an international relations class to Ethiopian cadets from the nearby Imperial Ethiopian Air Force Academy. I was allowed to develop my own curriculum and to select the material for my classes. Much of it came from the library at Kagnew Station, although a fair amount came from old weekly US news magazines such as Time, which I'd collected from fellow officers. I was being very carefully monitored by a very officious older officer who gave me the impression that if I went too far in advocating for a freer society, I'd be swooped up and locked in with the emperor's lions.

Finally, as my 18-month tour was ending, the NCOs in my unit held a farewell dinner for me at the NCO Club. They presented me with a large elephant tusk with a brass insert, which thanked me for my service. On the other side of the insert, it said, "future general Marvin Moss." They perhaps had more confidence in me than I had in myself.

The officers I worked for in Asmara were a depressing lot. Some of them reached the point of being ridiculed by junior officers for their lack of leadership and inanity. The enlisted personnel also had little respect for them. My commanding officer, despite my dedication and, I believe, stellar performance in both positions, wrote mediocre efficiency reports on me, which, in those days, was a major blot on my record. I believe they were, in fact, jealous of me and the high esteem the troops had for me and actually resented my integrating myself into the local Italian and African communities. This later became one of the reasons I terminated my military career.

Again, I'd plotted the most ingenious way to get back from Ethiopia to the States. It involved a three-week trip through much of Europe, followed by passage on an American Line luxury liner, the <u>SS Atlantic</u>, from Genoa to New York. I never could figure out why my military colleagues were not taking advantage of such opportunities. I flew to Athens and took a boat tour of some of the most interesting islands, including Mykonos, Delos and Santorini. I flew from Athens to Vienna, where I stayed in a charming B&B in an apartment in the middle of the city.

The first evening, I was eating dinner in a stube in the Alt Stadt when in the usual tradition, the Ober seated a young man opposite me at our two-seat table. He seemed a bit flustered and naïve about ordering. I asked him if he spoke German. When he answered, I instantly knew where he was from by his accent. I then asked him, "Where are you from in South Africa?" He was appropriately astounded and then asked me how I'd deduced his origins. I told him I was a trained spy and knew the accent from my travels in his country. He was on his way to Berkley to graduate school in economics. I ordered for him in German. Thus began one of Marvin's most bizarre and fascinating evenings. We went to several beer and wine stops, drank far too much, and were having a ball. We ended up at the central Domplatz in front of the Stephensdom, the cathedral. It was now raining, and I had with me the umbrella my B&B lady had lent me. At that time, this Platz was the hub of strolling prostitutes, who were also carrying umbrellas. I challenged several to an umbrella duel, which I won, but left my borrowed umbrella with great gashes. At 3 a.m., my South African friend and I were sitting on the curb saying our goodbyes, when he opined, "If all Americans are like you, I'm not sure I'll survive there." I went home, paid her for the damaged umbrella, and left the next morning on the Donau-Dampfschiff, the Danube steamer headed upriver toward Passau, Germany.

My room on the overnight trip to Passau was tiny. When I went to bed, I discovered my room was just above the engine room, so I slept very little. The next morning, we passed the famous Melk Monastery overlooking the river. Its library is one of the most spectacular in the world. On arriving in Passau, we could not disembark right away due to flooding on the three great rivers (the Inn, the Ilz, and the Danube) that converge there. My principal motivation for going there was the great organ in the Baroque St. Stephen's Cathedral. It and the Moller organ at the West Point Protestant Chapel (which my maternal grandfather helped install) vie for the title of the world's largest church pipe organs. The next morning, I attended the daily concert on this great instrument and visited the university, which is noted for its high percentage of foreign students. Passau is, to my mind, a great example of a mid-size German city off the beaten path that is sadly neglected.

The next goal in this wonderful trip was Munich. My purpose there was again music, including attending the annual Munich opera fest, held by the Bavarian State Opera at the Nationaltheater and on a stage in front of it. Many of Wagner's greatest operas, including Tristan and Isolde, had their world premiere in this noble opera house. I got to hear Richard Strauss' Der Rosenkavalier and Verdi's Un Ballo in Maschera. The trio in the last act of Rosenkavalier is, to my mind, among the greatest ensembles in all of opera. My trip was now taking both longer than I'd anticipated and costing more than I could probably afford, but I was determined to forge ahead. After three days in Munich, I went by train to Bregenz, Austria.

I have been a great fan of Bregenz for many years since my first visit in 1961. In the summer months, it hosts the Bregenz Music Festival with the Vienna Symphony Orchestra, the lesser-known of that city's two great orchestras. The city has a beautiful setting on the Bodensee, or, as it is known in Switzerland, Lake Constance, one of the largest inland freshwater lakes in Europe, with the foothills of the Tyrolean Alps in the background. The lake borders Austria, Germany and Switzerland. The venue includes a small opera house and an enormous stage built out over the lake. I stayed in a gemütlich Gasthaus near the lake, which specialized in local game dishes. The highlight of the stay was a performance of Swan Lake on the floating stage. In the end, when Prince Siegfried and Odette die for their love, they actually depart in this production in a giant boat that sails into the sunset surely one of the niftiest ways to enter paradise. Wagnerian in its dimensions and impact. It was one of the most pleasant stays in this entire voyage into hedonism.

Realizing I had to get myself to Genoa to catch the ship, I made a stop in Milan. I'd just finished reading Luigi Barzini's "The Italians" in Asmara before departing. This book, published in 1964, offers probably the most detailed description of the Italians as a people and the reasons they have been a mecca for travelers from elsewhere for hundreds of years. Among other things, it describes the Italian fascination with and love for official documents. I found a small hotel just across from the Milan train station, and when I presented my official passport to the clerk, he exclaimed, "Oh, Signore, un passaporto officiale." He was so awed that he put me in the largest room in the hotel and opened the then-closed restaurant for me to dine there all alone. It was both funny and unpleasant.

I finally wound up in Genoa several days before the Atlantic was to sail, and I spent the time exploring the Centro Storico, the ancient seaside quarter of the city, which was buzzing with every kind of human activity possible, from Punch and Judy shows to jugglers, flame swallowers and prostitutes lolling on the steps of the duomo. I loved the complexity of the scene and the apparent lusty participation of those who lived and worked there. Finally, I boarded the Atlantic, which was on its way back to New York after an extended Mediterranean cruise.

Due to the fact that the Army was paying my fare, I was assigned to a tiny windowless room with another man, a very gay schoolteacher who was sweet but rather uncommunicative. I had to take the upper bunk because I was younger and spryer. The trip was again memorable. The first night at the bar, I met a very overweight Jewish lady from Boston who announced she was the "junk queen" of that city. She was sporting a diamond ring the size of Manhattan. She promptly fell in love with me, which meant I was going to have to spend the balance of the voyage avoiding her. We stopped in Nice, Barcelona, Gibraltar and Lisbon on the way. As we neared the Azores, we received a message that a sister ship had a seriously ill passenger on board and was requesting that we rendezvous at sea to transfer the patient to our ship, since we had a doctor and a clinic. We met, and it was fascinating to watch the transfer take place in a rolling sea. Our detour caused a one-day delay in our arrival in New York.

After a week or so with my family, I went to Washington to scout out an apartment since I was next being assigned to the Defense Intelligence Agency as an analyst on Africa. I found a cozy third-floor one-bedroom walk-up in a townhouse in Foggy Bottom, along the Whitehurst Freeway. At that time, my friends Barbara Wilson and Irma Ireland were living in a tiny cottage on Locust Lane in Glen Echo. Irma was a very sporty type and was deep into rock climbing, which is where she met Barry Bishop, the leader of the first group of Americans to climb Mt. Everest, who was a frequent guest at the cottage. Our group included Chet and Saone Crocker, Joe and Bettye Pegues, Martin Hardy and later the

Palestinian sisters, Nuha and Nural Abudabbeh, and Theo van Vooren from Belgium.

Chapter 10
Defense Intelligence Agency

My DIA office was at an old WWII base in northern Virginia called Arlington Hall Station, replete with long, temporary buildings dating back to the war. The cast of characters in the African section was both diverse and odd. There was Radmilo Trianovitch, a charming old Serbian man with a strong accent, who wore a heavy woolen coat even when it was 90 degrees outside and fell asleep at his desk every afternoon; Barry Wickersham, who had just completed a master's degree in African studies at Indiana University and became a life-long friend and squash partner; Paul Holtz and a quite bonkers Irishman named Bob Burke. Bob smoked a pipe and would visit me at my desk while smoking, and would blow on his pipe instead of drawing, spreading live ashes all over my papers. He was very weird. He found out I liked classical music, so he would come to me, stand there silently, and then, in a loud voice, declaim "Buxtehude." Dietrich Buxtehude was an obscure Austrian composer of the 17th Century, and I'd made the mistake of telling Bob I liked his compositions.

I found our work there tedious, irrelevant, unfulfilling and generally useless. One of my roles was to write the Free World Air Intelligence Brief on some of the countries I covered. I even had to write a report on countries like Chad that had no air force at all.

A few months after I arrived, I drove to our office early in the morning to see that my building was on fire. I was silently praying that the whole thing would be consumed in an act of immolation, like the one in Gotterdammerung. Perhaps epitomizing the silliness of it all was a briefing on Ethiopia I was asked to give to Air Force Maj. Gen. Grover Cleveland Brown, the deputy DIA commander. Halfway through the briefing, I began to discuss the racial makeup of Ethiopians, and when I described them as being of Hamitic origin, he interrupted me to say, "They have to be negroid because I saw they have kinky (he pronounced it "kanky") hair." Barry Wickersham, who was assisting me with my graphics, and I managed to stifle a laugh.

In early 1967, I was transferred to the DIA office in the Pentagon, which was charged with preparing the daily intelligence briefings for the Joint Chiefs of Staff. I was covering the entire continent of Africa, but was later asked to take on both Africa and parts of the Middle East. Most of the Joint Chiefs' briefing officers were field-grade officers (majors and above). I was still a captain when I began briefing them. One of my triumphs during this period was my legendary "Pink-footed Booby" presentation. The Navy had begun preliminary talks with Britain to build a naval supply base on the Indian Ocean island of Aldabra, which happens to be a major breeding ground for the pink-footed booby and the great Indian Ocean sea turtle. When the typically besotted ornithologists in England got wind of the proposal, they began protesting at our embassy in London. The Chair of the Chiefs, hearing this, asked me to look into this, leading to my lecture. When I started out, General Wheeler asked,

"Captain Moss, why are we receiving this information?" I replied that he had requested it. They sat silently and restlessly through the breeding habits of this lovely bird. Finally, I felt that I had accomplished something useful for the national security of the United States.

The chief of the Africa/Middle East Section of DIA was Navy Captain Murphy, who had been monitoring my work with the Chiefs and evidently been impressed with it. The week before the June 1967 war in the Middle East broke out, he called me in and told me that he wanted me to be DIA's briefing officer for Secretary of Defense Robert McNamara. I was stunned, since this position would normally be filled by a Lt. Col. or higher, and I was unfamiliar with the armed forces' force structure potentially involved in the war. I had no choice but to agree. I began studying all available sources in preparation. When the war broke out, I was brought up to McNamara's office by his military aide and introduced. I could see that he was a bit surprised both by both my youthful mien and my junior rank. At that time, I had the highest possible security clearances, including several whose names were themselves classified. I was working in my windowless office 12-13 hours a day. After a few presentations to the secretary, I was asked to brief the Deputy Secretary, Cyrus Vance, and the Chief Counsel, Paul Warnke.

Perhaps the most interesting part of that assignment happened on the third day of the war. I was called to the secretary's office very early in the morning because he was about to go to the White House for a meeting with the president and the National Security Council. As I was about to finish my briefing, he asked me if there was anything else I thought he needed to know before leaving. I replied yes. I told him that I thought the Israelis had broken through the Egyptian lines on Sinai and were headed for Suez. He seemed puzzled and asked me where I'd gotten that information. He was even more startled when I responded, "from the front page of today's New York Times." He asked whether I thought the paper had more accurate, up-to-date information than our agents in the Middle East, and I again responded yes. As I returned to my office, I was unsure whether I'd done the right thing; however, by then, knowing the forces in play in Sinai, I was fully confident that I was correct. It turned out I was.

In September 1967, I was selected by DIA to take a two-week trip to visit our Defense Attache Officers in West and Central Africa, including Senegal, Ivory Coast, Ghana, Nigeria, Cameroon, and Chad, and to wind up in Paris. The mission was headed by Colonel Luther Evans, Jr., accompanied by a civilian analyst, Bob Matsco. I was delighted to be back in Africa and to be once again in many of the countries I'd visited during my studies. It was an exhausting trip but well worth it since in each country we were briefed by the Ambassador and his principal staff.

One of the things that surprised me as a result of my work in my various positions at DIA was the overwhelming influence the Defense Department had on the intelligence community and the relatively little credence given to others, including the intelligence arm of the State Department. At meetings to develop new intelligence estimates on specific countries or areas in Africa, usually held at the CIA, it was the position taken by me and other analysts from DIA that tended to prevail. I was disappointed that the diplomatic side appeared to be woefully underrepresented and not particularly respected. I assumed that the war in Vietnam was partially responsible for that situation.

In late 1967 and early 1968, I'd become more disillusioned with the war in Vietnam and began protesting it on weekends, knowing full well, in light of my official position at the Pentagon, I was perhaps placing myself at some risk. In late February 1968, I decided to take another of my monumental trips. I flew to Mexico City, toured all the majestic ruins around the city, rented a car, drove up Mt. Popocatepetl while picking up some American mushroom heads on their way to harvest on the mountain and wound up at the chaotic carnival in Yucatan. From there, I flew to San Francisco to stay with old friends from Asmara, and finally spent four days skiing in Aspen. By the time I got to Aspen, I was flat broke and had to get up early in the morning to eat most of the continental breakfast before the other guests arrived. During all of this, I'd become quite tan and had grown my mustache. When I arrived back at National Airport, Barbara and Theo were waiting to pick me up, so I decided to test them. My appearance had changed remarkably. I walked right past them without their even recognizing me. It was also on this trip that I had my first active gay experiences.

To say that 1968 was a year of crisis is a gross understatement. With the assassinations of Bobby Kennedy and Martin Luther King, our major cities were aflame. At one stage, I left work at the Pentagon in the late afternoon, and as I crossed the 14th Street bridge, I could see parts of the city burning. I was also feeding breakfast to some of the National Guard troops stationed along the Whitehurst Freeway each morning. In August, the March on Washington was taking place. I initially was reluctant to attend for a variety of reasons. In the end, I went. I hooked up with a group from a Lutheran church in Connecticut and marched to the Lincoln Memorial, where we heard the historic "I have a dream" speech. I was very happy that I'd decided to attend.

It was at that time that I'd decided that being gay in the Army was not a future with any stability or positive prospects, so I went to the Army personnel office to put in my resignation since I'd now fulfilled all my obligations, including my graduate schooling. The other motivation for my resignation was that there was now great confusion about my career path. My involvement with intelligence had now, in many ways, preempted my Signal Corps identification, and I was not looking forward to spending the rest of my Army career in the bowels of the Pentagon. I was shocked when I was told that West Point graduates and regular army officers were no longer permitted to leave the service without a tour in Vietnam (I later realized this was probably illegal). I then chose to do the one thing that would allow me to leave the Army. I volunteered to go to Vietnam and requested that I be assigned to a combat unit.

In October 1968, I was promoted to the rank of major at an office in the Pentagon. I was 31 but looked like I was around 20. With my newly installed oak leaf clusters on my shoulders, I was proudly walking down one of the Pentagon's endless corridors when I was stopped by an Army colonel. And then the age-old question popped up once again, "How old are you?" I told him, and he just walked away shaking his head in amazement.

I was required to have a physical before I left, so I reported to the infirmary in the Pentagon concourse. I had to undress and put on one of those incredibly stupid gowns that sort of meet in the rear. I was in great shape because I was playing squash several times a week at the Pentagon Officers Athletic Center. I was standing in the middle of the examination room when the doctor, a very handsome young major, entered. He looked at my charts, asked me to disrobe, and then said to me while staring at my body, "Major Moss, you are amazing. You're 31 years old and have the body and face of a teenager." All of a sudden, I realized that his interest in me was more than medical, and I wondered what would transpire during the balance of the examination. I was especially looking forward to the hernia and rectal parts. Nothing happened, but I again was thinking how odd and exciting it would have been to be seduced in the center of the Pentagon. I also found it slightly amusing that, in order to go to Vietnam, I had to pay all the parking tickets I'd accumulated over the years for parking in illegal spaces at the Pentagon.

My penchant for taking extravagant trips to and from my various assignments continued. I bade farewell to Mom and Ira at National Airport and could see on her face the anxiety she had about this venture. I flew to Chicago and took the classic train trip from there to California on the Zephyr, crossing the Great Plains and slowly ascending the Sierras on the way to San Francisco. The trip lived up to my expectations. I stayed several nights at an inexpensive hotel in the city and then reported to Travis Air Force

Base to fly to Vietnam. Most Vietnam War veterans will tell you they flew there on Continental Air Lines, on leased planes, and so did I. The stewardesses were middle-aged women who were very solicitous. My plane flew from California to Hawaii, to Okinawa and on to Vietnam. We were served the same food for the entire duration of the 15-hour flight. Throughout my life, I'd always been looking for particular situations that seemed to me grossly out of kilter with reality, and in that list I would include landing in Saigon with my earplugs in, listening to Brahms's Second Piano Concerto.

Chapter 11
Vietnam 1968-1969

As requested, my assignment was with the Second Brigade of the 101st Airmobile Division, the Screaming Eagles, with its headquarters just north of the historic city of Hue. The 101st had been badly battered during the Tet offensive especially in Hue. The experience of flying from Tan Son Nhut in Saigon to Hue was another unexpected one. We were flying on a C-130 Hercules, the workhorse of the Air Force. When I got to the plane, we loaded it through the tail. It was fairly empty until many buses arrived, carrying ARVIN government troops, their families, and their livestock. When we took off, we were all sitting on the floor, and infants, goats and chickens were crawling all over me. I rather enjoyed it.

Landing at Hue, I was met by the Brigade personnel officer who made sure my 45 pistol was loaded and ready as we drove north in a Jeep to Landing Zone Sally, the headquarters of the Second Brigade. LZ Sally was on the plains, amidst rice paddies and small villages, with towering mountains to the west. I was billeted in one of the typical wooden buildings so hastily constructed to accommodate the troops. I received a thorough orientation and met the Brigade commander, Colonel John "Black Jack" Hoefling, an impressive West Point graduate who was rumored to be a great field commander, a reputation I discovered later was well deserved. I was in charge of all communications for the Brigade, including with division headquarters and our three battalions. I had a Signal Corps company commanded by a captain to carry out our mission, which reported directly to me.

In the first few months, I discovered that with my troops routinely doing their work well, I had very little to do. After pondering this situation for a spell, I went to Black Jack and asked him to think of other ways I might be useful to him. He had obviously been observing me and my budding relationship with some of the junior officers. My reputation had again preceded me, with many knowing of my background, including as a briefer for Secretary McNamara and the Joint Chiefs. We had a very serious conversation. He said he thought I might have reservations about the war. I agreed with him that I did, but said I was there to do my job regardless of my feelings about the cause. He accepted that. He then asked me to be his informal liaison with the Brigade's junior officers. He also guessed that I was quite good at writing, so he asked me to do two additional things. He would train me in base defense, then put me in charge of ensuring that all his units were complying with best practices and of giving him written reports on their status. He also gave me the responsibility of investigating and reporting on all friendly fire incidents where American troops had either been wounded or killed by other Americans. I readily accepted. This conversation was the one that made my remaining months in Vietnam both challenging and emotionally draining.

In the early months, we officers dined in a large tent each evening for a rather formal meal. The commander, deputy and senior staff sat at a high table. The rest of us sat wherever we could find a seat. Almost immediately, a young infantry captain who was the assistant operations officer began sitting next to me at all our meals. His name was John Pape. He'd been seriously wounded two years before, recuperated for many months and then requested to return to Vietnam with a combat unit. He was very different from me. However, it became apparent that he was fascinated by me and wanted to learn from me. He was constantly quizzing me about my studies, my travels and my experience in the Pentagon. Despite our difference in rank, we became friends.

I believe it was in December that I went out to take a shower one morning (an occasionally amusing experience, since the water in the giant overhead container from the Perfume River was anything but perfumed and offered not just water but toads and other best-unnamed critters). As I entered, an extraordinarily handsome, well-built young man stepped out of the shower. He looked at me and said, "You wouldn't happen to be Major Moss, would you?" I said I indeed was he. Then he said, "Well, I'm your new roommate." My immediate thought was that this was going to be difficult since I was going to be seeing this gorgeous young lieutenant pilot naked at least twice a day. We became very close over the ensuing months.

I'd also met some of the young warrant officer helicopter pilots, whose jobs were potentially among the most dangerous, since they regularly flew in and out of fire bases in remote dangerous areas. One was Brad Stillman, who'd been studying English at the University of Virginia. How did I meet him? I was in our tactical operations center (TOC) listening to the daily briefing when it struck me that much of what I was hearing was errant nonsense. I was walking up the stairs muttering to myself, "Honi soit qui mal y pense," the motto of the Order of the Garter, when Brad, coming down the steps, said, "Dishonor to him who thinks ill of it." I looked at him and said, "We are going to be friends."

We were sporadically receiving rocket and mortar attacks, mostly at night. One night, I could not sleep and was smoking beside our hootch, facing the mountains, when I saw a flash and knew it was a rocket headed our way. I yelled "Incoming" and most made it to the sandbags before it went overhead and landed in the nearby ARVIN camp, killing dozens of soldiers and their families. On my expanding list of weird experiences was the night we gathered in an open field to watch "The Sound of Music," which I found dreadfully boring, when we started receiving mortar fire. It was the only time I felt relieved to have been reprieved by mortar fire. Frequently, at night, we could hear B-52 bombers dropping their bombs on the Ho Chi Minh Trail during the Rolling Thunder operation, an apt name.

In early March 1969, the brigade combat assaulted into the A Shau Valley, a lush and beautiful area closer to the Laotian border. A few days after the assault on Fire Base Whip, Col. Hoefling asked me to fly out to check the communications and ensure the defenses were properly set up. We were still in the rainy season then. Brad Stillman flew me out to Whip in a loach, the small two-seater helicopter with the plastic bubble front. It was very cloudy, and we could not find a visual on Whip. Brad took the chopper up through a hole in the clouds, found the fire base and deposited me there. The weather then socked in, and I was trapped on the first fire base in the valley.

Soon after I arrived, a captain, commander of one of the artillery batteries on the hill, came to me with his radio. It was Black Jack telling me that I was now the senior officer on the fire base and therefore "king of the hill" or the one in charge. I quickly called all the officers together and told them that (some looking disgruntled that a Signal Corps officer was in charge). I checked the perimeter and found the defense set up satisfactory. I arranged to have my own radio to communicate with the other units when needed. I dug myself a very wet foxhole. I, of course, had only the uniform I was wearing, no toiletries, and no changes along with me. Throughout the night, I walked the perimeter, checking on things (it was easy to stay awake since I was surrounded by two artillery batteries firing defensive fires all night long for other fire bases). I was there for three days before being rescued.

A few weeks later, the brigade moved its headquarters temporarily from LZ Sally to Whip. I went out a bit earlier to dig myself another defensive trench and to organize a more sophisticated communications setup to include a telephone system using a rig borrowed from the Corps' signal battalion. I added to my list of most bizarre situations right after that. Late every afternoon, a huge CH-47 helicopter arrived bearing a sling load of beer for the troops. It usually carried Budweiser. One afternoon, the helicopter was about to land when the troops observed that it was unloading Pabst Blue Ribbon. A protest (really, almost a riot) ensued. No wonder we lost the war. We were there for over a month when the Colonel (White Owl was his radio call sign) called me into his tent. He told me, "Major Moss, I'm sending you back to base camp for a break." I told him I wanted to stay. He said, "You have to go back for the simple reason that you stink." I laughed because, of course, I hadn't had a shower in over six weeks, so away I went.

Back at LZ Sally, I met Lieutenant McCready, my beautiful hooch mate. We had a few beers at the officers' mess. The Catholic chaplain also lived in our building, so we then got into his communion wine, which was stacked in the refrigerator. Once back in our hooch and all alone, Bob put some romantic music on the radio, came over to me and asked me to dance with him. He and I were dancing cheek to cheek when I realized that if caught, we'd both be canned. I remember that moment so vividly. Not because I was dancing with an Adonis, but because I realized that, under unusual circumstances, a straight man needed to find an emotional connection and outlet, however possible, with another human being. Soon after returning to Whip, our command sergeant major was playing Russian roulette with his own revolver when he shot and killed himself.

A series of events pushed me into high gear with my new responsibilities. The first was one of the most tragic. I was notified early one morning that another American had killed five Americans during an overnight ambush along a canal north of our base. The man who'd fired all the shots was a young sergeant who happened to be in charge of the operation. The rules of engagement for an ambush are really quite simple. The parties to the ambush are settled in their positions before dark and are required to stay there until first light the next day. If they see anything moving during the night, they automatically engage the targets. The sergeant sent five of his platoon to a position off to his right. He was on duty in the middle of the night when he saw movement and opened fire, killing all the moving targets, who just happened to be the other half of his ambush. What happened evidently is that the ranking man among the five had not been told the rules, panicked and started moving his group back to the main party, not realizing they would all be killed.

I met the sergeant who was absolutely traumatized and sobbing, and had to take him out to the site on a chopper. I had him describe in detail what had happened, and I realized it was not his fault because the leader of the other group was new in the country and had not been taught the rules of engagement. I flew him back to Sally and took him to the headquarters building. I met White Owl and briefed him on what had happened. He agreed with my analysis, and I asked him fervently to get the sergeant out of the country immediately and to provide him with psychiatric counselling. The last thing the young NCO said to me was, "I don't know how I can live with this." That night, I too was traumatized.

A few weeks later, 13 of our soldiers were killed on Firebase Tomahawk in the A Shau by a Vietnamese sapper attack (sappers were deadly they wore only shorts, approached an American fire base starting at sunset by crawling on their backs, snipping their way through the barbed wire defenses and late at night attacking. The only weapons they had were bandoliers of hand grenades strapped to their bodies. Once inside the perimeter, they were deadly and suicidal). My pilot flew me to the base in the late morning. As I got off the helicopter, bullets zinged across in front of me, coming within feet of hitting me. A sergeant grabbed me and threw me against a steel container. I said to him, "That sounds like an M-16 (our American standard rifle) and not an AK-47." He agreed. I reached for my rusty 45 pistol. He took one look at it and said, "Sir, you can put that away. I have this under control." In fact, I, the officer in charge of friendly fire incident investigations, was shot at for the first time in Vietnam by Americans. It seems a patrol had been sent out without notifying the troops on the hill, and the firefight ensued until the mistake was discovered and ended.

The 13 GI's.bodies were lined up by the helipad. The first body I looked at had a helmet with "Why me?" written on it. I had to move away quickly in order to check my emotions. I had the company commander walk me through what had happened the night before. He'd sent a patrol out to an adjacent hill late in the afternoon, always a mistake because the troops then don't have time to prepare adequate defenses. He had also not arranged for defensive artillery fire around the newly established position another huge mistake. That is precisely what happened. The entire platoon was slaughtered in just a few minutes in the middle of the night by sappers, and there was nothing the main base could do to defend them. In addition, the captain had to be held responsible for the fiasco of the friendly fire situation that morning, which almost cost me my life. I put him on the helicopter with me and went directly to White Owl. I told him what had happened and implored him to relieve him of his command at once, which he did. This was another shattering experience.

It was our sister organization in the 101st, the Third Brigade, that Major General Melvin Zais, the division commander, ordered to take a hill near the Laotian border in early May 1969. The purpose of the assault on this high, solitary mountain was to cut off the infiltration of North Vietnamese supplies and soldiers down the Ho Chi Minh Trail. The battle began on May 10th with a seasoned North Vietnamese unit holding a commanding position on the summit. For four long days, the American forces, with some South Vietnamese units, fought in rain and cloud cover, which limited air support, to take the hill. Hundreds of Americans were killed or wounded. The press named the battle "Hamburger Hill" as a result of the devastation. The American forces finally reached the summit only to abandon it some three days later. I happened to fly into a fire base near the battle to check on some communications equipment, only to discover that it contained a triage field hospital. Helicopters with the wounded were arriving every few minutes. I fled the scene because I did not want in any way to hinder the treatment of our troops. Hamburger Hill has appropriately become a symbol of the futility and cost in lives of the Vietnam War. A few weeks later, the troops in the 187th Infantry Battalion, the first outfit to lead the charge, placed a bounty on its commander, an offer to pay anyone in the unit to "frag" or kill him.

Hamburger Hill, in many ways, demonstrated why we were doomed to lose the war and eventually leave the country. Not only was the battle planned for a period of the year when air support was likely to be marginally available, but there evidently was no plan for the long-range occupation of the mountain once it was conquered, thus obviating the very purpose of the assault to permanently interdict Vietnamese troops coming south along the Ho Chi Min Trail. To abandon a hill won with immense loss of life just three days later defies comprehension. Worse yet, the battle further degraded the units' morale and sparked rising antipathy toward the commanders who instigated it.

My friend, Captain John Pape, had been given command of an infantry company at his request, something I believe he'd always dreamed of doing. His company at that time was stationed at a very remote fire base in the southern part of our command, and I decided to visit his unit, check his defenses and communications, and enjoy his company. My roommate flew me there in a loach through spectacular countryside with waterfalls crashing out of the mountains. Captain Pape was waiting for me at the helipad and enthusiastically took me on a tour of his fire base. As we approached the helipad for my departure, he seemed to me to be quite suddenly a bit morose. Just before I boarded my helicopter, he saluted me and said, "Goodbye, Major Moss, sir, I may not see you again." He then shook my hand and held it for a long moment. I knew immediately that he had just telegraphed to me in that brief exchange a premonition of his death. I'm not sure how I knew that, but it was certain in my mind. The contrast could not have been greater between the two of us: he a warrior, brave, strong, courageous and committed. I, a skeptic and critic of war and one untested in battle. Despite that, the nexus between us was deep and strong, something I never really understood but treasured. I got on the helicopter, and Lt. McCready took off. I asked him to circle the helipad, where I once again waved goodbye to my friend. I almost immediately began weeping silently. Bob asked me what was wrong. I told him I could not talk about it. A month later, John and his unit were sent south to join the First Marine Division. There, he and his radio operator were killed in a mortar attack. When this was announced in the officers' mess that evening, I had to get up and leave and walk for hours around the air strip in deep sorrow. I know it is difficult for people who have never been in a war to understand the kind of unspoken communication that passed between John and me that day, but I know it happened. These things are not rational, but then again, neither is war.

I was flying in a chopper somewhere near our bases in the A Shau when I suddenly began to have severe lower abdominal pain, which had happened twice when I was in Asmara, resulting in hospitalization. They never found out the cause, treated me with antibiotics, and the pain and fever quickly disappeared. I had my pilot fly me to the division hospital at Camp Eagle, where I was admitted. They must have given me morphine because I fell into a deep sleep at once. When I began waking up, I heard the GIs on both sides of my bed cursing their officers and railing about how stupid they were. At that time, they thought I was one of them. Then the orderly placed my nametag, including my rank, at the end of the bed, and the whole ward instantly fell silent.

In July, I was finally permitted to leave Vietnam for a week of R & R (rest and relaxation) and chose to go to Taiwan. I caught a flight from Saigon filled with officers and enlisted men going to the same destination. There were five young officers from one of our infantry battalions on board the plane with me. One of them knew me. He asked me where I was going in Taipei, and I described the mountain spa inn where I'd made reservations. I did not tell them that it was also a brothel (perhaps I didn't need to). They all wanted to tag along, and I agreed. We took taxis from the airport up steep and winding roads to the beautiful spa. They had placed me in the largest suite, with a living room, dining room, and a bedroom, as well as a private spa on the floor below. After we checked in, the hostess asked if we wanted women escorts, and we all said yes (me rather reluctantly, but I'd now put myself in a position where saying no might have raised questions). Ladies of the night came on the equivalent of their Vespas roaring up the mountainside. As the senior, I got to choose first and took the most attractive woman. We made love several times (I was actually surprised how enjoyable it was) and soaked in our private pool for hours. I'd made arrangements for all of us to go to dinner at a neighboring restaurant -- both officers and ladies. During dinner, the date of one of the lieutenants was sitting next to me and said, "My man is so horny, I'll not get to sleep for the next 24 hours, so watch what I'm about to do." I watched. She leaned over, kissed her lieutenant passionately and slipped a sleeping pill into his beer. He was out of it in no time. I, of course, toured the national museum, which contains the greatest collection of Chinese art in the world, almost all of it taken from mainland China by the Nationalists in 1948-1949. I also bought some beautiful antique porcelain.

In the summer of 1969, an armored battalion was put under our operational control and was moving into our command area when the colonel asked me to go inspect their defenses and ensure they met our standard operating procedures. I was flown out to meet the unit. I was greeted by the commander, a Lt. Col. and his operations officer, who happened to be my West Point classmate, Nick Krawciw (later Major General Krawciw). They were staying buttoned up in their tanks at night and had dug no defense entrenchments around the perimeter. I told them what needed to be done. They immediately refused. I went back to my chopper, radioed White Owl and told him the situation. He said, "Just wait there. I'm on my way." When he arrived, he told the battalion officers to follow my orders right away and that he would return in the afternoon to ensure they had done so. I was proud of him and myself for ensuring that the unit was well prepared for any eventuality.

For my work as DIA briefer to the Joint Chiefs and Secretary McNamara, Captain Murphy recommended me for the Joint Service Commendation Medal, a new medal for distinguished service while in a joint service position. In Vietnam, we were visited by the Corps commander, Lt.Gen. Richard W. Stillwell, a highly respected combat officer. It was arranged for him to present awards and medals to officers and enlisted men during his visit. I was the highest-ranking man being honored and was to receive the lowest-ranking medal, the Joint Service Commendation Medal. Others were being decorated with silver and bronze stars and other important recognitions for their heroism and service. At the end of the ceremony, General Stillwell asked me what the medal was and why I was receiving it. He was rather astonished at my answer. Later, I was awarded the Bronze Star for my efforts in the A Shau campaign.

Lt.Gen Richard Stillwell presented me with the Joint Service Commendation Medal April 19. 1969

In late August, I was transferred to the 501st Signal Battalion, the outfit providing communications for the 101st. I was very unhappy about that, given my strong identification with and commitment to the officers and men of the 2nd Brigade. The commander was on some kind of mysterious medical leave in Thailand and had been gone for months; consequently, two West Point graduate majors were in charge. It took me only a few days to see that the unit was in terrible shape, that drugs were rampant among the troops and that morale was at rock bottom. Even worse, the two majors were sending relay units into the jungle without infantry support or proper defensive preparations. I tried my best to right the situation, but was stymied by both of them. Since I'd already submitted my resignation from the Army, which had been accepted, I could be brutally frank with them, although they both outranked me. It was a difficult time for me. To my travail was added the revelation that some West Point graduates are inept and should never be placed in command positions. As I was preparing to go home, I asked the division personnel office who the incoming battalion commander was to be. It was none other than my terrific commander in Germany, Lt. Col. Richard W. Smartt with two tt's. I warned my colleagues what was coming. I found out when Corky, his nickname, was arriving in Saigon and delayed my departure for the States long enough to meet him and fill him in on what he faced up north. He was very grateful. We stayed great friends for the rest of our lives until he reposed in 2020.

I was appalled at the condition of the 501st Signal Battalion during my 3 or 4 months with it. It was without direction and leadership, rife with heavy drug use, extraordinarily low morale, marginally capable of carrying out its mission to provide communications between the division and its brigades, and suffering from racial animosity. It was difficult for me to gauge whether this situation was typical of other units in our division or the exception; however, I felt, then and now, that it was far more likely representative of what was happening elsewhere in the 101st Airmobile Division. It is hard for me to imagine what happened to these combat units subsequent to my departure in 1969. What I am describing here reflects an absolute nadir in the

US Army and provides much fodder for dissecting the reasons we had to flee the country in 1975. At the same time this was occurring in Vietnam, there were race riots in the barracks in the 7th Army in Germany.

The war also started what had not really existed in the country before a widening chasm between laborers and the increasingly educated urban elite, with laborers generally supporting the war, and the elites vehemently protesting it. In other words, the war in Vietnam had not only an enormous impact on domestic politics in the US at the time but also on the future direction of the nation's politics well into the 21st Century.

It also challenged and changed the Army. The leadership in Vietnam was viewed by the troops there and in the US as being feckless and dishonest about what was actually happening in the war. The appointment of General Creighton Abrams as the new commander finally ended the incredibly inept leadership of William Westmoreland, who, to my knowledge, never set foot in our operational area and thus surely had no clue what was happening in this key area of northern South Vietnam. The war, in essence, undermined the very basis of an effective military -- order, discipline, and respect for the officers and NCOs who lead the troops. The result, years later, was the move to an all-volunteer army, which, of course, has its own problems and challenges.

In a footnote to my experience both in Ethiopia and in Vietnam, I now realize that I'd had a profound effect on some of those who served under me, including my troops in the desert in

Ethiopia and, later, junior officers in Vietnam, including Brad Stillman, Captain John Pape, Lt. Bob McCready, and others. I was surprised in 2003 to receive a letter from a man then employed at the UVA Hospital, asking if I was the same Major Moss he'd known in Vietnam. It turns out he was the commander of a small, highly classified unit at LZ Sally while I was there in 1968-1969. It was an intelligence unit intercepting Viet Cong communication. I tried to visit it but was told that I did not have adequate clearances. The lieutenant checked and discovered that I had a Talent Keyhole clearance far above top secret (I was, incidentally, the only officer at LZ Sally with such a clearance). I was then permitted to enter and spent many hours trying to lift their spirits since they were virtually isolated from the rest of the camp. The letter was an expression of gratitude for what I'd done many years before. I tried to call him, but he'd moved away without leaving any contact information. I mention this only because I did not recognize at the time that my subordinates believed I was an effective and compassionate leader.

My final departure was in so many ways a recapitulation and sad culmination of my year in Vietnam. I was flying from Saigon to Travis with a stop in Alaska. Because I was the ranking officer on the plane, I was made the troop commander responsible for ensuring the troops were accounted for throughout the flight. I was watching the enlisted personnel boarding the plane, most of whom were from the First Infantry Division, which had been in desperate combat in an area near the Cambodian border for many months. As they filed on, I saw in their faces the shock of war and their sullen, silent, vacant stares. I kept thinking how unfair it was to send these shell-shocked young men home to their families when, in fact, their loved ones were completely unaware of the heartache and trauma they'd just experienced. I could only have wished that there had been some period at Travis where they could have had a decent transition and some expert counselling, but alas, it was not to be.

I took the bus from Travis and stayed in the same hotel I'd been in a year earlier. I asked the concierge if there was a great place to have a cocktail with a view of the Golden Gate and the bay. He suggested the Marriott, which had a bar on its top floor, fitting my description. I was alone in the bar and had just settled in a comfortable chair overlooking the view when the bartender, a young man, arrived. He looked at me and said, "When did you get back?" I knew immediately what he meant, and I replied, "Is it that obvious?" And he said, "Yes. It's the look of a man liberated and at the same time a bit confused and disoriented." He told me drinks were on the house. I was home.

It was obvious to me after these 12 months that my own experience during the war had borne out my reasons for opposing the war. I believe that some senior officers, such as my first Brigade commander, Col. Hoefling, also recognized the futility of what we were doing. I had the distinct impression that what was actually happening in the field was not being accurately portrayed to the headquarters in Saigon. Those in charge in Saigon were essentially blind to the lack of progress and to the extraordinary courage and commitment of the North Vietnamese and the Viet Cong.

After my return and well into the 1970's, I continued to read about the antecedents to the war, including David Halberstam's "The Best and the Brightest," which delves into great detail about how a group of exceptionally talented individuals at the highest level of government got almost everything wrong about Vietnam. I had a tangential connection to one aspect of his book. He wrote about the great Red Scare and the dismissal of many of the old China hands as a result of McCarthyism and the fall of mainland China. My neighbor, while I was working at the Pentagon, was Robert Service, a foreign service officer and the son of John Service, who'd been fired from the State Department for predicting exactly what eventually happened in China. He was just one of the "old China hands" dismissed. As Barbara Tuchman wrote: "History has recognized them as having been right. For having been right, many of them were persecuted, dismissed, slowed or blocked in their careers, with whatever damage done to them personally outweighed by damage done to the Foreign Service of the United States."

When I returned to my family in Hagerstown and my civilian friends in Washington, I now recognize that I was emotionally drained from my experience in Vietnam. My family and friends would ask me about it, and as I recall, I responded with vacuous generalities and never told anyone, including my family, what I'd actually experienced there. I think that is because I did not know quite how to answer their inquiries or how to explain the depths of my feelings, I had about the futility and the horror of the war, including foisting that airplane full of traumatized GIs on an unknowing and probably indifferent society. Everything I experienced in Vietnam only increased my strong opposition to the war.

The Vietnam Memorial -- Marvin's mistake. Jan Scruggs, a young veteran of the war and a Maryland resident who initiated the idea of the memorial, visited me frequently, seeking my support and that of the senator for the memorial. I was adamantly opposed to the idea, thinking that it was going to honor the war itself, one of the most difficult eras and errors in American history. When the memorial was dedicated on November 13, 1982, Senator Sarbanes decided to attend and insisted that I go with him. It was a brutally cold, stormy day. I was still unconvinced until after the ceremony, I looked up the name of John Pape, my friend in Vietnam, went to the panel with his name, placed my hand on it and began to weep and realized how wrong I'd been all along about the memorial.

Chapter 12
The 1960's

I was at a social gathering here in Fluvanna County, my home, some 10 years ago, during which a local band and vocalist were performing. A song started, and a lady next to me asked, "Is this your favorite song from the 1960's?" I looked at her and said, "I've never heard that song in my life." She did not believe me until I told her that I'd lived abroad for almost the entire decade of the 1960's. From my graduation from West Point in 1959 until 1970, I spent almost 7 years outside the US. In many ways, being away from my country during this period was a double blessing in that I was living and studying in Europe, Africa and Asia and learning what I could of the world away from home, plus it gave me a unique opportunity to experience the enormous changes taking place in our society from a different perspective.

Each time I returned to the United States from my various stays abroad, I was surprised by how quickly things had changed during my absence. In one case, miniskirts and men wearing tight pants on the streets of Georgetown were a slightly erotic manifestation of change. Another was the nascent idea of women's liberation. The other major change, from my perspective, was an increasingly and probably enduring rise in the average citizen's negative view of government, undoubtedly engendered by the war, the chaos resulting from the civil rights movement, the rise of Black power organizations, and the growing bifurcation between the north and the unhappy south. One of the major blocs of power in Washington had been the solid Democratic tilt of the Deep South, which, after the Johnson administration's civil rights and voting rights legislation, was rapidly evaporating.

It was the decade that encompassed almost everything including the assassinations of President Kennedy, Bobby Kennedy and Martin Luther King, passage of two historic civil rights bills, the conservative takeover of the Republican Party, a sweeping immigration law, escalation of the endless war in Vietnam, the Freedom Summer in Mississippi, utter chaos during the 1968 Democratic National Convention and destructive riots in the inner cities of almost all our major urban centers. One does not have to tarry over this mixed roster of events to conclude that American society was moving in directions which had never before been experienced or contemplated, including, among other things, a then undetected rise in consumerism and unbridled individualism and a silent and gradual march away from our collective understanding of the meaning of the American experiment.

Perhaps one of the best descriptions of where we were post-World War II and how we arrived at our present woeful state is by David Leonhardt in his 2023 book "Ours Was the Shining Future." After detailing the remarkable improvements in American life over 25 years after the war, he shows how a stagnation in living standards has become the defining norm. As the NY Times review of the book states, "Life expectancy has declined, economic inequality has soared, and after some progress, the Black-White wage gap is once again as large as it was in the 1950's." Leonhardt explains in great detail the battle between two competing forms of capitalism: one that envisions prosperity for most and one that serves the individual and favors the wealthy. It is the transition between the moderate capitalism of the post-war period and our present approach that has made this situation possible.

In the present era, faced with a political party in the grip of a single madman and the weakness of the Democratic Party, it is highly unlikely we will have the courage or fortitude to address these problems. Leonhardt points out the pivotal role public investment in infrastructure, education and health plays in solving these problems. President Biden has recognized this and enacted major legislation to address our environmental and technological challenges; however, funding for early education programs for our toddlers remains well below that of almost all other developed nations.

The book also outlines the rise of what he calls "Brahminism" or "Brahminist economics." This is a result of the bifurcation of American society and its electorate, whereby the highly educated and generally more urban college and university graduates have migrated to the Democratic Party and are generally advocates of economic capitalism while largely ignoring the people of fly-over America and their increasing alienation from the New Deal consensus on the role of government in general in our society. This has been exacerbated, of course, by the Democratic Party's endorsement of a social agenda that eludes much of middle

America, which is struggling to maintain a standard of living they feel is increasingly unstable and threatened.

This has been a major change from the time I started working on Capitol Hill in 1971, although the potential for this political earthquake was probably already building, even then, though most of us, including me, were generally unaware of it. The changes I observed have had a monumental impact on our politics and lives in the 21st Century. It was this decade that fundamentally changed American society and has, to my mind, been the basis of the political turmoil we are now experiencing.

Perhaps the decade is best summed up by a poem by Peter Schjeldahl, "My Generation." Among other things, it includes: "Vietnam/Drugs/Civil Rights/Rock/Watergate/ (in that order?) /Are the flowers of history/that have left my generation/its peculiar battered silhouette."

Chapter 13

Free at Last

I found the transition to normal life more daunting than I could have ever imagined. Home in Hagerstown on leave with my mother and Ira, I made a decision that I was not going to tell them the more harrowing aspects of my service in Vietnam a pledge I've kept for many years until recently. I was also very uncertain about my future since I was about to resign from the Army and had no real plans. I'd been increasingly concerned that the Vietnam War was an endless quagmire and that it had been driven by politicians with some support from clueless military officers such as General William Westmoreland, which piqued my interest in the possibility of getting involved in Democratic politics. I decided to move to Washington to begin this new phase in my life and found an elegant one-bedroom apartment on Capitol Hill.

In late December 1969, I was officially separated from the Army at Ft Meyer, VA, where I collected all my back pay, received my decorations and my release papers. I had saved my entire salary from the year in Vietnam, which had been invested at 10% interest, and I still had a small but valuable stock portfolio, so I was solvent. Just before Christmas, I went to the annual holiday choral celebration at the national cathedral. During the intermission, I ran into Barry Wickersham and his future wife, Anne. I had to blow my nose and pulled out my handkerchief, which was a tattered, dirty remnant from the war. Barry and Anne looked at it and broke into laughter. I also renewed my friendship with all the people I'd known over the years in the city.

I spent several months deciding what to do. I drove Barbara, Theo and some other friends to the VW dealership in Arlington in my mother's Cadillac. When I arrived, I jokingly told the salesman I was trading in the Cadillac and wanted a new VW for all my friends and me. In reality, I bought another VW bus since I'd loved my camper bus in Germany. It slowly dawned on me that there was an upcoming congressional election in Maryland's Sixth District and the likely Democratic candidate was Goodloe Byron, whose parents had both served in the House in the early 1940's. His father, William Byron, had been killed in a plane crash in Atlanta, and his wife, Katherine, was appointed to fill out his term. The Byron family was wealthy and owned the Byron Tannery in Williamsport, which produced much of the high-quality leather used in the Postal Service's mail bags. I decided to give joining Goodloe's campaign a shot, and through friends in Hagerstown, I was introduced to him and his wife, Beverly.

I drove to Frederick each weekday on my bus to the Byron headquarters, where I was given a variety of responsibilities under Beverly Byron's tutelage. Beverly also came from a distinguished family. Her father was a TV executive and, during World War II, had been stationed in London as Eisenhower's naval aide, with the rank of Captain. His wife was a friend of Mamie Eisenhower and was then living with her at the Wardman Towers in Washington, one of the city's most exclusive addresses.

That is where it is rumored that they both started drinking a bit excessively. Unlike Eisenhower, Captain Butcher divorced his wife and married a woman he'd met in London. Beverly attended the Cathedral Girls School, which is where she met Goodloe, a student at the adjacent Saint Alban's. Beverly remained a close friend of the Eisenhowers for the rest of the president's life.*

*Beverly Byron related this story to me. She and Goodloe were one morning preparing breakfast in their pajamas in their house in Frederick when there was a knock at the door. She opened it, and there were President Eisenhower and Mamie. They were driving from Camp David to Washington when he asked the Secret Service to detour to their house in Frederick. She invited them in while both of them ran upstairs to get dressed.

It was during this period that I became actively gay, frequenting the many bars in the city. At one stage, I was dating an Air Force captain and began introducing him to my straight friends, so I was publicly coming out of the closet. This was liberating for me in that I no longer had to hide my being gay in fear of being forced out of the Army. In doing so, I saw the reaction of some of my women friends, who had been attracted to me and were obviously disappointed that I'd taken myself out of the marital pool. The period of my return from Vietnam in 1969 until the mid-1970's was one of increasing visibility of gay men, especially in major cities such as Washington and New York. I felt quite comfortable with this newfound freedom and only regretted that I was still hiding my true self from my mother, something I have since deeply regretted.

In November 1970, Goodloe was elected to the House of Representatives, and he hired me as his legislative and projects director. We had an enormous swearing-in party with folks from all over the 6th District coming to celebrate, including my proud mother and Ira. She was finally relieved that I'd found gainful employment with a possible solid future in store. The 6th District was and is one of the most conservative areas in Maryland, reflecting the settlement in Western Maryland of Pennsylvania Dutch and Scots-Irish from Pennsylvania. It is very much like the Shenandoah Valley of Virginia. In Goodloe's class, entering the House were Parren Mitchell, the first Black congressman from Maryland; Paul Sarbanes from Baltimore and the redoubtable Bella Abzug. I love the story of her dramatically entering the House chamber with a large hat on when the long-time Doorkeeper, a southerner of the first order with the wonderful name of Fishbait Miller, approached her. He went up to Ms. Abzug and said, "Ms. Abzug, you can't wear a hat on the floor," to which she replied, "Fuck you, Fishbait."

Chapter 14
House of Representatives and Stephanski

Our office was on the 7th floor of the Longworth House Office Building. We had interesting neighbors, including Abzug, whose staff frequently fled to my office in tears after being berated by her; Bob Eckhart, a liberal Democrat from Houston who wore pork pie hats and rode a bicycle to work; and a Democrat from the West who was always listed as one of the 10 dumbest members of the House. Relationships with all liberals, conservatives, southerners, urbanites, ruralites, Democrats, and Republicans were cordial. Every month or so, we would have a floor party with a piano, which Goodloe could play by memory. At one such party, I asked the one listed among the dimmest if he could play the piano, at which point he held up his hands. He only had two fingers on each hand since he'd once been a laborer on the oil rigs and replied, "What do you think?"

My role became central to the office. I was not only a legislative assistant but also a legislative correspondent, a projects officer, and a liaison with our field staff. I almost always traveled with Goodloe on his constituent visits to the various sections of the district, taking notes, getting to know the locals, learning the political landscape in each county, and making many new friends in the process. I also became close friends with many on our staff, including Doris Solomon, Chris Moore, Mary Ellen O'Brien and Joyce Harrell.

The Maryland congressional delegation was chaired by Senator Charles "Mac" Mathias, a liberal Republican from Frederick. I attended all the delegation meetings, which met once a month, and played an active role in their deliberations. I smoked rather dramatically at the time and noticed Congressman Sarbanes looking askance at me for that; however, I could also see that he respected my comments. I was quickly learning about the various grant and other programs available to local jurisdictions and began outreach to them, encouraging them to apply for grants with our assistance. Many of them had never used such programs before, so the opportunity was a revelation to them.

Goodloe was becoming more conservative in his voting and refused to take a position against the war, which I continued to oppose. He was well aware of both my experience in the war and the reasons for my opposition. I was becoming increasingly disillusioned, mainly because it was quite clear that I, as his legislative director, had no influence whatsoever on him or the positions he was taking. He won his 1972 and 1974 elections, in which I was very active, including fundraising, by wide margins, so I kept pointing out that his popularity gave him some leeway in his voting. After the 1974 election, I decided to consider leaving the staff in 1976, at the end of his term.

My six years of working in the House were great training for my future work in the Senate and later during my retirement. I'd essentially taught myself the whole range of federal programs that could assist a rural community, as most of Maryland's Sixth District then was. I only realized later that my outreach to the counties in Western Maryland had sparked local governments' interest in applying for and using federal programs they'd never known about. Although I was very fond of Goodloe and Beverly, I had the feeling they never really understood the scope of what I was accomplishing. A few years later, after I had become chief of staff to Senator Paul Sarbanes, Goodloe's new staff director called me to say they had had to hire three people to replace me.

In 1973, I bit the bullet and bought my first house in Washington, a 14-foot-wide townhouse on 5th Street SE on Capitol Hill. It was in a great location close enough to my work that I could walk to the Longworth Building. I began buying art and other items to decorate it and started creating a garden in its deep back yard. I loved being in that neighborhood with its tiny Jewish corner grocery store, the Eastern Market within walking distance, and the restaurants and bars on 8th Street by the Marine Barracks. I was now regularly frequenting the gay bars and movies and having casual relationships along the way. But still, no one to love.

That began to change dramatically in June 1974 when I met a young man at the gay flicks. After a few minutes, he asked me, "Do you have some place where we could go?" I found him attractive and did something I very seldom did I invited him to come home with me. I did not even know his name until he got on my bus and introduced himself by saying, "Hello. My name is Steve." I was 36 years old and had not had a steady beau since the Air Force captain. We had drinks and went to bed. The next morning, he talked about himself and his ambitions and asked me detailed questions once he discovered that we were both Vietnam veterans (he as an enlisted Marine). He'd been very active in the Vietnam Veterans Against the War and had demonstrated with them many times, so we had that in common. He indicated almost right away that he was a student of theology, had graduated from a seminary high school, and was ultimately interested in becoming a priest. I recognized that he was very different from many of the men I'd met before, was serious, intelligent and to me quite charming. I fed him breakfast and, at his request, drove him to a Ukrainian celebration at the statue of Ukraine's national poet, Taras Shevchenko. I repeated my name and suggested he call me. He gave me his full name, Stephen Juli, and told me he lived in suburban Maryland.

A few weeks later, I looked him up in the phone book and called the listed number only to hear that the phone had been disconnected. I was disappointed and regretted not getting better information from him. Not too long thereafter, he called me, and I arranged for him to come to the house for drinks and for dinner at a nearby restaurant. With that, we began seeing each other regularly. He, unlike me, was very shy and unused to large social gatherings with people from diverse backgrounds, so at first, when I would have friends over to the house to meet him, he would break out in a cold sweat. Gradually, he became accustomed to my friends from Belgium, England, Morocco, Rhodesia and Palestine, as well as many others from less exotic climes.

During this time, my friend from Rhodesia, Marshall Baron, came frequently to visit his sister, Saone, and spent many evenings with us. Steve loved his wry Borsch Belt sense of Jewish humor and his amusing tales of life in unsettled Rhodesia. We both loved classical music and spent hours listening to Mahler and discussing our favorite recordings. It was also obvious that he was heading into a serious bout of drinking, which manifested itself one evening when he was standing on his head in my living room in his bikini and fell into the fireplace, which fortunately was not lit. I was trying to help him in any way I could. Steve relished his company. On one of his last visits, Saone asked me to let Marshall stay at my house since they had young children, and his drinking was becoming a problem. I agreed. He died tragically and far too young when he overdosed in his studio in Bulawayo and died. I spent hours consoling Saone and the family. A wonderful part of my life had also suddenly disappeared, irrationally.

After a year, Steve was coming over every day and staying overnight, leaving early in the morning to get to work at Catholic University, where he managed its print shop. I knew by this time that this was a serious relationship and was likely to last. One of the clinchers was the first Christmas together when he lugged my present, the huge multi-volume Oxford English Dictionary, the whole way from Union Station to the house. Suddenly, he announced that he was giving up his apartment and moving in with me. I was, at first, rather shocked because this meant a more permanent commitment on my part, but I also thought it was the best way to normalize our increasing love for each other. Finally, we said, "I love you" to each other. A joyful proclamation.

In the spring of 1975, I was travelling in Europe with my friends Barbara and Theo in their car. I wanted to see Prague very badly. We entered from Austria, and at the border had all our international newspapers and magazines confiscated by the Czech guards. I loved Prague immediately. Among other things, we visited the Jewish quarter with its large cemetery, which was almost in the center of the city. There was a very moving video of the Jews taken from the city to the camps where they organized orchestras, plays and other cultural activities before being shipped off to their deaths. I kept thinking about the loss of entire families and the incredible talent they represented. While we were there, we knew there was a good chance Saigon was falling. I tried to find a German newspaper to no avail. I finally got in the car and listened to Bavarian radio in German to find out the news.

We decided to go skiing in the Czech Tatra Mountains, and to do so, we had to visit a dusty office in Prague to get a travel permit. We drove north of the city only to discover near the immense Skota automobile factory, there was lots of snow, but it was covered with black soot from the nearby industries. When we arrived at our destination, we had a shot of a local liqueur and fled back to Prague.

Among my many friends at the time was Nuha Abudabbeh from Palestine, who had just married Abdelkader Kadiri, the first secretary of the Moroccan Embassy. He called me and asked if I could do him a favor. Princess Lalla Latifa, the crown prince's wife and future queen, was coming to Washington, and he wanted to show her a typical American home, so he selected mine. We agreed. So, on the appointed day, the crown princess and her extensive entourage arrived at our tiny house in mid-morning and were shown our less-than-splendid abode. I thought it odd that a Moroccan princess was being introduced to a household inhabited by a gay couple. It was also obvious in a few minutes that her real interest lay in her next stop Neiman Marcus, so her stay with us was blessedly brief.

Mom and Ira came for visits from time to time, and I had to hide the fact that Steve was not only my partner but also a full-time resident at my townhouse. Once she called when I wasn't home. He answered the phone and then pretended to be a plumber working on the house. I don't think she was fooled. Later, there was a terrible fire at one of the gay baths, killing 8 gay men. It was on all the evening news programs. Within minutes, mom was on the phone asking whether I was ok. Steve once again reiterated his view that our secret was out and that Mother knew I was gay. Unfortunately, I never did tell her about the most important man in my life, and I have regretted it ever since.

Steve had been an activist against the war and a member of Vietnam Veterans Against the War for several years. In December 1971, he and a small group of mostly stoned protesters took the ferry to the Statue of Liberty, hid in the arm and torch until the park was closing and then announced to the departing National Park ranger that they were taking over the statue and the island. They were really quite tame protestors. They cleaned up the area around the statue and were assiduously making sure they did no harm to the site. Their photo appeared the next day on the front Page of the New York Times with the hippy Steve front and center. They surrendered peacefully and were not arrested.

Steve on the front page of the NY Times, December 27, 1971

When Steve's parents found out about this escapade, they were both aghast and intensely embarrassed. He did not particularly care. I raise this point to illustrate his determination to see something through once he set out for a specific purpose.

It was probably in 1976 that Steve received a box of brownies from one of his Vietnam buddies. He asked me to eat one, as did he, before we headed out to dinner at a gay restaurant in midtown. During dinner, he began to tremble uncontrollably and was sweating profusely. I too was getting hot spells and was dizzy. I managed to pay the bill, get him into the car, take him home, and put him to bed, where he shook all night long. I was holding him and unsure what to do. I thought of taking him to an emergency room, but that would have exposed our drug intake. He finally fell asleep. The next day, I asked him to ensure that this never happened again. He, of course, agreed and kept his word thereafter.

That summer, Steve and I took a long trip west, starting in San Francisco. We had an open relationship as far as sex was concerned and spent some time on the beaches beneath the Golden Gate Bridge, a notorious cruising area. We then traveled north on US 1 to Muir Woods National Park and Point Reyes National Seashore, which I found breathtaking, with its dairy farms and cows along sheer cliffs, the sea pounding below, and seals basking in the sun. Steve had long hair and looked every bit as if he really belonged in San Francisco. I was still working in the Byron office and probably looked like a government nerd. We also visited Fort Ross, the tiny traditional Russian stave church that marks the southernmost penetration of Russian settlers in the early 19th Century.

A year or so after he moved in with me, his identical twin, Basil, who was a teacher in the Ukrainian Catholic Church, came for a visit. He took readily to me, and we became friends almost at once. I attended his ordination to the priesthood in 1977 at the Ukrainian Cathedral in Philadelphia. I knew, ever since I met Steve, that at some stage he too would want to be ordained into the priesthood of his church, which celebrated the same liturgy as the Orthodox but commemorated the Pope rather than an Orthodox prelate. The possibility of being separated from him was always at the back of my mind. I'd just read a book about the meaning of love, which emphasized that the ultimate test of love was giving each partner the freedom to fulfill his or her dreams (doesn't that seem very 1960ish?). I took that to heart and decided I would support whatever decision he made, no matter how sad it made me.

Chapter 15
Stephanski and My New Community

As I commenced work in the Senate, Steve (or from now on to be known by my favorite nickname for him Stephanski) was living with me at my Capitol Hill townhouse. It was in 1977 that I decided to buy a larger, more glamorous house in the up-and-coming Logan Circle neighborhood. I bought a recently renovated 4-story house on Rhode Island Avenue. It had a living and dining room, kitchen, and powder room on the first floor, a master bedroom and bath on the second, and two bedrooms and a bath on the third floor. It also had a one-bedroom apartment in the English basement. I began renting out both the 5th Street house and the apartment. Stephanski loved the old house because it was the first real home he'd had, and he was not particularly thrilled with the new abode. Logan Circle was then a dicey area with lots of drug dealing and prostitution, much of it right in front of our house. One of our favorite prostitutes was a hefty young woman with exceptionally large legs, whom we dubbed "Miss Thunder Thighs."

I very quickly became involved with the Logan Circle Community Association (LCCA) and made quite a reputation after completing three community gardens in the neighborhood. The first was a small plot on the then notorious corner of 14th Street and Rhode Island Avenue, an overgrown patch of weed trees and tall grass which the local prostitutes used as a tricking site. I designed and installed a garden there consisting of many shrubs with large thorns to deter the nightly assignations. I called it my "prickly patch for the pricks" garden.

My next effort was far more grandiose. On 11th Street, there was a very large, ugly Pepco substation with a one-acre lot behind it, enclosed in a tall security fence. I met with Pepco's public relations team and convinced them to allow me and my committee to design and landscape a garden on their property, which would enhance both their building and the streetscape. They agreed and began cooperating. One of my friends in the neighborhood was a landscape architect who designed the garden pro bono. I also saved us lots of money by arranging for the company excavating the new Air and Space Museum on the Mall to deposit its soil in the new garden, saving them money as well. We planted flowering trees outside the fence, daffodils on the mounds, ornamental trees inside and a wildflower meadow. I contacted Henry Mitchell, the venerable garden writer for the Washington Post, and asked him to visit; he wrote a glowing article about this community beautification effort. Later, I designed and planted another small garden on public space on 15th Street. After all of this, I was elected President of the LCCA and served for 4 years in that capacity.

My nephew, Nathan, and his friend, Isaac, both 13, arrived from Maine to spend a week with me. They were completely naïve about life in the big city, but quickly became accustomed to and amused and fascinated by the comings and goings of the ladies of the night. At 5 pm on a Saturday, I told them it was time for the weekly fire, and we dared not miss it. They had no idea what I was talking about. You see, every Saturday at 5 pm, the city's firetrucks pull in front of the large apartment house opposite my place with sirens blaring. It just so happened that the building was the home of dozens of attractive prostitutes. They would dash into the building and a half hour later emerge smiling. We sat on my stoop, and exactly at 5 pm, the fire engines arrived for their weekly saturnalia. My youngsters loved it. They got into serious trouble when they attempted to board their flight home with their suitcases stuffed with fireworks. They later asked their parents if they could come live with Uncle Bud. I wonder why.

It was then that Stephanski decided to fulfil his long-held desire to be ordained in the Ukrainian Byzantine Catholic Church, and I began to accept that our separation was now inevitable. I knew how difficult this decision was for him, given the increasingly deep and abiding love we felt for each other. My many friends had now become his as well. At his ordination to the priesthood in 1978 at the Ukrainian seminary in Stamford, CT, in attendance were my friends Theo and Barbara van Vooren from Belgium; Joe and Bettye Pegues, Black friends from grad school; Abdelkader Kadiri, first secretary of the Moroccan Embassy and his wife, Nuha; and Nuha's Palestinian sister, Nural. We were all staying for the weekend with the Pegues at their Southport house. After the liturgy and ordination, I said my tearful farewell to him, not knowing when or where I would ever see him again. I was overcome with grief.

On the way home, I began composing in my mind what would become the first great gay opera written in the style of Richard Strauss. The plot was simple. Two men fall in love and have a passionate, enduring affair. One of the two decides to become a monk in an Orthodox monastery. The other reluctantly accepts this despite the agony it brings him. It all culminates in a magnificent scene before the walls of a monastery, where the two lovers (one a tenor, the other a baritone) sing a passionate farewell duet as the monks' rising chants cascade over the walls and blend into a mighty crescendo. I can still hear it in my mind.

Our period of separation was trying for both of us. He first went to a Ukrainian monastery in the mountains of Northern California. He typically threw himself into the services and routine of monastic life and probably overdid the Lenten Great Fast, losing dozens of pounds. My only communication with him during this period of about six months was an occasional letter. He finally came to visit the Rhode Island Avenue house. After that, he was very unhappily assigned to several Ukrainian parishes as an assistant pastor in Amsonia, CT, and Buffalo, NY, where the rectors made it quite clear they did not want him there. It was a very sad and confusing time for him and me as well. Eventually, he had his own parishes in upstate New York in the villages of Amsterdam and Little Falls.

It was during this time that he was at the movies one evening when he was attacked by a young teenager wielding a hammer. He was struck in the head several times, was admitted to the hospital and was there for several days before being released. I was praying for him and was very worried. Stephanski visited his attacker in prison after he was sentenced and forgave him, an action I enthusiastically endorsed. After a month or so in the middle of a very cold winter, I went up to see him. We took a trip to Lake Placid and a few other places in the Adirondacks. He was very silent, obviously depressed and unhappy. I was even more worried about him than ever. From time to time, he would fly from Syracuse to Washington to stay with me. I was always a bit nervous when I met him at the airport, thinking perhaps we'd become somewhat estranged in the interim. That fortunately never happened.

1983 marked the advent of AIDS and the fright it engendered in the gay community. Most of us changed our behavior immediately when the cause was definitively identified and toned down our sexual explorations. The reaction of the Reagan administration to this new deadly disease was at first one of denial, and once the proximate cause of the scourge was identified to avoid active governmental participation in finding treatments to deal with it. This Reagan reaction was a direct holdover from the "Lavender Menace" of the Cold War days, and the delay in searching for anything to counter AIDS was clearly responsible for the loss of thousands of lives. Several of my friends in Washington succumbed to it, including an exceptionally talented young artist.

A few times, we would rendezvous in New York, where we stayed at the Incentra Village House on 8th Avenue in the West Village. It was there in 1984 in the Bishop's Suite that we found a new and more intense way of expressing our love for each other.

Chapter 16
Chuna Yupik Eskimo

My friends, Irma O'Brien and her husband, Danny, had been schoolteachers and salmon fishermen in Dillingham, Alaska, on Bristol Bay, perhaps the world's most important source of coho salmon. We'd been friends for many years, dating back to my graduate school days in Washington. Irma called me and asked if I would host a local Yupik artist, whose works were about to be in an exhibit of native North American art at the Canadian embassy. His name is Chuna McIntyre. Chuna was not only an artist and educator but also the creative director of a group of traditional Yupik dancers, which had performed all over the world. He has become the leading expert on Yupik Eskimo art including as a consultant to the Metropolitan Museum of Art and the Smithsonian Institution.

Chuna arrived and was utterly charming. He showed me the native costume he was to wear and his giant seal-skin drum as part of his dance routine, so I invited him to come to my office in the Senate to perform. My coworkers in the Sarbanes office, being fully aware of my penchant for the odd, were delighted as he arrived and danced while explaining much of the history of his Yupik people.

On a Friday evening, I was anticipating the arrival of my friend, David Dethero, from Flat Rock, NC. David is a great friend. He is a very traditional southern man given to conservative ideas of behavior and protocol. That afternoon, I received a call from an old high school friend who was in town and wanted to invite me to dinner. I accepted. I asked Chuna if he would stay at the Rhode Island Avenue house to greet David. He agreed. When David arrived, he rang the doorbell, and Chuna, wearing his full feathered dance regalia and carrying his huge drum, answered the door and said, "Hello. I am Chuna Yupik Eskimo." David's response was, "Oh my God, Marvin has done it again." They got along famously.

Here is an original artwork by Chuna he gave to me in thanks for hosting him. It is entitled: "Snowy Owl."

Chapter 17

Marvin's Travels

This trip took place in 1975. I was traveling with my Belgian friends, Barbara and Theo. We arrived in Rhodes, checked into a hotel in the city center, and began exploring the maze of ancient streets with their charming stone houses and unusual lintel decorations.

Several days later, in our rental car, we circumnavigated most of the island, including a trip over the mountainous central spine and arrived in the classic Greek site of Lindos. Lindos is most famous for its Greek temple, built in 300BC, but the site also includes a large acropolis that has been only partially excavated. The temple of Athena, situated on its prominent hill, offers stunning views over the cobalt-blue sea. The Acropolis, which rises above the town of whitewashed houses with doors painted in every conceivable color combination, was successively fortified by the Greeks, the Romans, the Knights of St. John, the Venetians, and finally the Ottomans. Near the crest of the Acropolis is the Greek Orthodox Church of St. John, parts of which date back to the 6th Century.

We parked our car, walked through the incredibly beautiful village and hiked to the summit. When we returned, we settled into a café by the bus station, had several glasses of wine and played Scrabble. It was now late in the afternoon. I was watching as all the tourist buses were departing. I'd also noticed that the only hotel was on the outskirts of the village and was far removed from anything authentically Greek. Pondering all of this, I suddenly suggested to Barbara and Theo that we spend the night there, but not at the hotel. They reluctantly agreed. I began asking in the village for accommodations, but almost no one spoke English. I then remembered that the Italians had occupied Rhodes until the end of World War II, so I thought of finding an older person who still spoke Italian. Very quickly, I found a man who did, and he took us to a house on one of the many side streets and introduced us to a woman who would put us up in two rooms. Her house was typical of Rhodes with a main entrance leading to a large central atrium filled with grape vines and flowers. She charged us the equivalent of 90 cents per room, including breakfast. It was one of the most charming places I've ever stayed.

That afternoon, I'd been reading my guidebook, which mentioned that on the outskirts of the village was the Porto Piccolo, by tradition the site where St. Paul set foot for the first time in the Hellenic islands. We walked there and sat in silence, looking at the small port with an entrance cut through the stone cliffs, when an unknown bird began singing a haunting, ethereal song. It seemed so appropriate for such a sacred place.

We went in search of a taverna for our dinner and found one near our rooms. After a hearty dinner, the taverna began to fill with locals who came to socialize and dance to traditional Greek music, a la Zorba the Greek. We joined in the fun and lost track of time. Around midnight, the taverna closed, but our newfound friends motioned us to follow them. They led us to one of the town beaches, carrying their boom box and lots of ouzo and wine. We danced on the beach until the wee hours of the morning, capping a day of extraordinary experiences.

The next morning, our kind lady at our overnight guesthouse handed each of us a string bag filled with a generous Greek-style breakfast. She then said to me in Italian, "Take your colazione (breakfast), go to the Acropolis and the temple, and watch the sun rising over the sea." We, of course, complied, enjoying one of the most serene, quiet breakfasts ever. There wasn't a single tourist in sight, which is exactly why I'd wanted to stay there after all the buses departed. It was 24 hours of sheer bliss.

On our return to the City of Rhodes, I went to a local park, which my gay guide said was a cruising area and met a very attractive young man, who, it turned out, was Italian, so we were speaking that language. Next to the park was the moat of the Pope's palace (why a Pope's palace on a Greek island? Because the Venetians had occupied Rhodes for many years.) In order to have some privacy, we climbed over a wall into the moat. We'd just begun getting acquainted and starting to undress when suddenly loud music and huge lights were illuminating the moat. Seated above us were 500 people on bleachers. We had instantly become part of the Son et Lumiere (sound and light) show. The Italian panicked and fled. I took a deep bow to my assembled fans, laughed hysterically and climbed back over the wall. An appropriate end to a few magical days in Rhodes.

In the 1980's, I traveled to Europe almost every year. I don't remember the year, but I was in Paris for a few days. Late at night,

I took a taxi to a rather swanky gay club called Les Nuages (the Clouds), located in Saint-Germain-des-Prés. Like all such French establishments at that time, it was filled with smoke from the Gitanes. It took me a few minutes to acclimate to the dark and the smoke and to find the bar. When I reached the bar, there was a single man hunched over the bar all by himself. He lifted his head for a moment, and voila, I was looking at Rudolf Nureyev. Even in that short glance, I could see that glorious face with its chiseled features, and even in relative repose, its power to sweep all before it. It was also obvious to me that he wanted to be left alone, so I moved away quickly. He was at that time the director of the National Opera Ballet, transforming it into one of the world's great companies. What struck me as both odd and interesting was that the other gay men there knew who he was but left him completely alone. Something that would never have happened in the US, where he would have been mobbed.

Chapter 18

The Three Grande Dames

It was probably a fortuitous accident of fate that the mothers of three friends arrived simultaneously in Washington, DC, and, through their children, managed to establish a most astonishing international friendship. The first was Josephine van Vooren, Theo's mother, who was born into a large Dutch family in a village near the Belgian frontier. She was one of 13 children. She was a widow whose husband had died many years ago. She came to DC to be with Theo and lived with him in his apartment for many months. The second was Nimet Abudabbeh, Nuha's Palestinian mother, who'd been living in Libya after the death of her husband. She was residing at Nuha's house. We always called her Madame Abudabbeh. Then there was my mother, Louise Moss Roth, who visited me frequently from her home in Hagerstown.

I've described them as the three grandes dames because that is exactly what they were in every possible interpretation of the adjective grandes. They were all imposing physically. Slightly overweight but still attractive, they had all led interesting and stimulating lives and developed strong personalities commensurate with their life experiences. They knew who they were and did not hesitate to express their thoughts and opinions.

Others and I organized a series of parties to which all the grandes dames were invited, including a promotion party and other less structured evenings. They, of course, had never met before. The chemistry between them was almost instantaneous and was a marvel to witness. They immediately gravitated toward each other and spent most of those evenings getting acquainted (and probably dissecting the various perceived indiscretions and lives of their beloved kinder). Nuha, Theo, and I were very delighted to see this and to understand how similar the lives of the three of them had been long before they ever met. I mention this simply because what happened was a tribute to three utterly remarkable women and their unique outlook on life.

Chapter 19
The Tundra Boys

I'd been invited in the early 1980's to join a group of Baltimore friends from the law firm of Gallagher, Evelius and Jones to go skiing on their annual trip to Stratton Mountain in Vermont. The principal organizer was Rick Berndt, the managing partner and a close political ally. Rick was a tireless organizer, and many of the skiers were young attorneys from his firm. Although most were much better skiers than I, I agreed. We stayed the first two years in February at the home of Frau Wendland, who, with her late husband, had built by hand a perfect replica of an Alpine chalet. She came from a wealthy and distinguished Dutch family, including her brother, Eugen Jan Boissevain, who married Edna Saint Vincent Millay. The loo walls were covered with her poetry. Her husband was German. Her son, Jan, skied with us and had a great influence on me, helping me relax and improve my skiing. After skiing, we had a cocktail hour while I played Shubert sonatas on her aging piano, followed by a delicious German dinner.

We then began a more vigorous and enterprising ski adventure by going each February to St. Anton, one of the charming villages in the Tyrolian Alps, "ski circus." We usually flew to Munich or Zurich to catch the train. We always stayed at the luxurious Alte Post Hotel, where we also ate most of our meals. We had a ski instructor with us at all times. In the villages of St. Anton, Zurs, Lech and St. Christoph, all connected by lifts and trails, there were over 92 lifts and countless alpine opportunities, most with a vertical drop of about 5,000 feet. Lech is where I'd learned to ski with my friend, Christa, in the early 1960's.

The group began to find me a most amazing spinner of yarns as well as a source of the most bizarre information. It started when I corrected a guide in a baroque church in Munich, telling her in German that she had the history of its leaded windows wrong. I think they were both charmed and a bit frightened of me. Since I was 15 to 20 years older than most of them, I was always called Uncle Bud and treated like the slightly addled eccentric uncle who showed up only for Thanksgiving. My reputation was enhanced when I skipped several years of the trip and, upon arriving at the Alte Post, Rick introduced me to the new bartender, Ben. Rick then challenged me to guess his nationality, and if I did so, I would have free drinks on him for the duration of the trip. I then asked Ben in German, "Koenen Sie mir sagen auf Deutsch "my house is green?" He responded quickly. I then said, "I now know your nationality." He and the others were flabbergasted. I said, "Here is my reasoning. You speak both English and German with a slight French accent. Your first name is Ben, which is a common first name in the Maghreb Morocco, Algeria and Tunisia. Ben is not common in Morocco. Most Algerians are tall and Lanky. You are short and stocky; "alors, Je crois que vous etes Tunisien, n'est ce pas?" He replied, "bien sur, mon ami." I was again stared at by my comrades with both admiration, incredulity and more than a bit of trepidation.

On one of my trips with the gang, we went to the top of the Valuga peak, the highest mountain in the Tyrol, and skied down to a lodge some 2,000 feet below for lunch. After lunch, the gang was ready to go, but I had to take a pee, so I went inside. When I came out, they'd left. I had no idea where we were or how best to get back to St. Anton, so I started off. Unfortunately, I wound up on a double-black Olympic run that was almost completely vertical. I used the mogels to turn on, but soon became exhausted. I finally reached a road in the middle of nowhere, but knew that eventually one of the many ski buses would be by. One soon came. I looked like a Yeti when I got on the bus. I was halfway between St. Anton and Zurs. The gang was waiting for me at the bar and said, "Uncle Bud, where the hell have you been?" They were unsympathetic when I told them my tale.

One final tale about St. Anton. There was a wealthy American who stayed at the Alte Post for the three months of ski season each year. The locals came to like him partly because he was a major contributor to the local Catholic church. He was so well respected that the Mayor of St. Anton, in his official garb and ancient sashes, convened a ceremony at the hotel and named him "honorary mayor of St. Anton." The next year on his return, the staff at the Alte Post became concerned that he'd not returned from the slopes at his usual cocktail hour. At the same time, the family of a young ski instructor also noticed that he had not come down from the mountain either. I'd noticed this instructor once before when we were going up on the huge gondola lift. This amazingly handsome blond young man entered in his ski guide uniform. I'd never seen another human being so beautiful. All eyes, both men's and women's, on the gondola were instantly on him. Only later did I discover that he used his beauty to his advantage. He was a "rent boy" for whoever, men or women, were willing to pay for his services. The town fathers became alarmed, alerted the night ski rescuers, lit up, started the lifts, and began surveying the entire mountain for the two. They never found them. They both skied down in the morning from the mountain shack where they'd stayed the night and were met by the hopping mad mayor and the kid's family. The mayor revoked his honorary title and forced him to contribute $30,000 to the local church. Interestingly enough, the young man was evidently not punished for his indiscretion.

One year, we departed St. Anton to return to Munich, where I'd managed to arrange to meet my friends, Senator Barbara Mikulski and Congresswoman Beverly Byron. We met them at the legendary Hoffbrau Haus for beer and laughs. They were attending the annual Munich Security Conference as part of the official US Delegation.

I relished these excursions despite being a relatively awkward skier, and I loved the company. On some trips, I would skip skiing and take the train down to Innsbruck or go to the next village with a book, eat lunch and return in time for drinks and our dinner. I read much of Lawrence Durrell's Alexandria Quartet during these interludes. At my retirement party in 1995, the entire ski gang showed up and, at my request, ended the ceremony with our traditional yodeling routine.

Chapter 20
US Senate

In December 1975, I left the Byron office after six years, not knowing what I would do next. I got a temporary real estate license, but disliked the idea of doing that for the rest of my life, finding it intensely boring and not at all challenging. Steve realized how unsettled and unsure I was about my future. It was the year Congressman Paul Sarbanes was running for the US Senate against the Republican incumbent, J. Glenn Beall, Jr., whose father had also been a US senator. They were from Cumberland in the far west of the state. Sarbanes began calling me each time he was headed to central or western Maryland to campaign, seeking my advice on whom to meet, folks who might host a reception for him, and other key information. He obviously found it helpful since he called me each time he was going west. He defeated Beall decisively in the general election after defeating former Democratic senator Joseph Tydings in the Democratic primary. I'd admired Sarbanes from the outset of his congressional service, including his stellar performance as a young congressman, given the awesome responsibility of writing and introducing the first article of impeachment against Richard Nixon. His background as the son of Greek immigrants and his education at Princeton, Oxford, and Harvard Law were also draws. I decided to apply for a position on his Senate staff.

To increase my chances of joining the Sarbanes staff, I wrote a lengthy paper summarizing his record on international and national defense issues during his six years in the House and delivered it to his then-chief of staff, Burt Wides. Meanwhile, from many friends in Maryland, I was hearing terrible accounts of the early months of the Sarbanes office, including failures to respond to elected officials and to correspondence. It was in May of 1977 that Burt called me for an interview. Burt had worked for both Phil Hart and Ted Kennedy in various capacities before being asked to head up the senator's staff. Burt called me and asked me to meet him at his Capitol Hill house. We walked to Eastern Market, a few blocks away. Rain had been predicted, so I brought my umbrella with me. Burt did not have one. We had breakfast at Eastern Market, which he made me pay for. By then, it was raining hard, so he took my umbrella and headed home, while I had to scoot the 6 blocks to my house in the rain. It was the oddest interview in my life. Evidently, I did fine since a few weeks later I was called to meet with Peter Marudas, Sarbanes' Greek mentor, and Nick Schloeder, a long-time campaign aide. I was concerned that the rumor that I was gay could impede my being hired, but if it was a concern, it was never broached.

In May, I was asked to meet with Senator Sarbanes in his office, where he offered me a position on his staff, although it was quite vague about what my role would be. I took it to mean I was in charge of projects and liaison with the state staff. Following the meeting and job offer, I had to tell him that I was headed for Belgium in a few days for the christening of my God-daughter, Priya. Priya and her sister were Indian babies whom Theo and

Barbara had adopted through Mother Teresa. Steve and I were in Antwerp and Amsterdam for almost three weeks before we returned to DC to begin my work. Steve was still managing the CU print shop.

My new office was to be in an old, dismal apartment building across from the Hart Senate Office Building. We had two rooms and a bathroom. The staff working there included Bruce Gilmore, who was in charge of projects; John Baron, a press aide; and a secretary. It became obvious to me in a day or two that the office was completely disorganized and dysfunctional. Yellowing local newspapers were stacked almost as high as a desk, files were stored randomly in the bathtub, and no one had evidently been in charge of this mess from the outset in January 1977. I announced that I was now the boss and expected them to follow my directions. The first weekend, I had the custodial staff deliver a trash truck to our suite and had them throw almost everything into it old newspapers, unanswered letters from local elected officials, and other documents. The trash truck was filled to the brim. On Monday, when they came to work, they were livid. I told them that, from now on, all correspondence from elected officials would be responded to within 48 hours, phone calls would be acted on immediately, and that I would review and sign all letters leaving our office. La revolution avait commence!

At the top, the office was even more confusing. In order to talk to Burt, you had to go through his secretary/assistant, Ingrid Vorhees, whom I promptly branded the Viking. It was obvious that Burt was essentially clueless about what was happening (or not) in the office. The senator was personally signing all correspondence, resulting in huge piles of old letters sitting on his desk. That backed up the entire legislative correspondence process and was clearly one of the causes of the office's dismal reputation among the public. As I was observing all of this, I began, in August, to think about ways I might be able to change the system subtly without rocking the boat or appearing to be operating above my pay grade. I met privately with the correspondents and suggested that we implement a system I called "selective deprivation." That is, we would begin slowly reducing the letters flowing to the senator's desk; I would review the rest and sign them. Finally in the end, only key letters on important issues would go to the senator. We began this program without consulting those seniors to me a bit of risky business to say the least. By this time, it was also obvious that the nexus between Burt and the senator was almost nonexistent. Burt was a legislative activist, and Senator Sarbanes was a cautious and deliberative man in his first year.

At the same time, I discovered that the state's staff had received no training or introduction to the programs that could benefit Maryland's 24 jurisdictions. I then organized a day-long trip to Philadelphia for the staff, during which we met and received briefings on the various grants and other programs administered by the Region III federal office there. I also explained the system I'd used in the Byron office to make these opportunities available to the counties. The senator's press operation was also moribund simply because it did not appear to be a high priority to him. By this time, my sub rosa meddling was becoming obvious to everyone and was received positively since the operation began to be both better organized and more effective.

In September 1977, Burt and the senator parted ways amicably due to an almost complete lack of a working relationship between them. In early October, the senator asked me to replace Burt and to work side-by-side with Peter Marudas, who was to be my co-chief of staff and the brains behind our political operation. Peter was unique - a Greek from Detroit with a degree from the University of Michigan and an unbelievably deep understanding and appreciation of the American public and its political thinking. He'd been the senator's friend and mentor for many years; a relationship I could not match nor even try to match. We worked together for 18 years without a hitch. My only problem from time to time was Peter's elliptical way of expressing himself. As one Baltimore politician who knew him well said, "Peter talks in digressions." We would have a long conversation, and when I went back to my desk, I had to say to myself, "What is it that Peter was trying to convey to me?" Sadly, Peter reposed in 2021, not long after Senator Sarbanes a great loss for so many people who admired and loved this exceptionally positive, intelligent and caring man.

The senator's committee assignments were also of interest to me Foreign Relations, Banking, Housing and Urban Affairs, and the Joint Economic Committee. Initially, as a junior senator, we had no staff on the committees, so my responsibilities included liaising with the Democratic staff of each committee.

Chapter 21

The Sarbanes Record

In lieu of a litany of my work in the Sarbanes' office, I believe a review of his major achievements would give a better understanding of his impressive record.

The Panama Canal Treaties

It has long been my contention that one of Paul Sarbanes' greatest achievements is one that has generally gone unacknowledged - the passage of the Panama Canal Treaties in March of 1978. The senator had been assigned to the Foreign Relations Committee's Subcommittee on Latin America despite his strong interest in other areas, including the eastern Mediterranean. It then became his duty to be one of the leads in the effort on the floor of the US Senate to ratify the treaties, which dramatically altered the future of the canal, its ownership and management. This was an arduous and thankless task in light of the conservative reaction and opposition to this diplomatic initiative.

President Jimmy Carter initiated negotiations on the bilateral treaties as part of his overall program to improve relations with our Latin American neighbors. His ambassador in Panama at the time was an adroit diplomat named William Jorden, who'd been a diplomatic correspondent for the NY Times before joining the

State Department. He played a key role in negotiating the treaties with the Panamanians. He visited our office frequently when Sarbanes became the chief deputy floor leader to Frank Church in the debate. There were actually two treaties under consideration. The first retained a permanent right of the US to defend the canal from anything that might interfere with its continued neutral service to ships of all nations. The second phase passed control of the canal to the Republic of Panama by December 31, 1999, including its operation and defense.

The treaties were highly controversial, with conservative organizations throughout the country calling for their defeat and issuing dire predictions that the canal would eventually fall into the wrong or enemy hands, totally ignoring the fact that the first treaty allowed the US to intervene to prevent such an outcome. Just before he began spending full time on the floor defending them, he did a series of town hall meetings throughout the state (very risky in that setting), and I went with him. In Cumberland, MD, a relatively conservative county in Western Maryland, his appearance drew a large and generally hostile crowd. He began slowly and carefully outlining the US history in Panama and the details of each treaty in a manner reflecting his Harvard Law training. It was a masterful job. In the end, many in the audience were not convinced; however, by the very nature of his presentation, he had silenced the vocal protests that would normally have occurred.

Once the treaties were laid before the Senate, he was spending many hours each day on the floor shepherding questions, blunting the opposition's more blatant exaggerations, and working with members of the Republican leadership to ensure enough of them voted to reach the magic number of 67. He worked closely with Frank Church, who later chaired the Foreign Relations Committee. Throughout, Church relied heavily on Sarbanes to address the more obscure technical issues inherent in the language. It was also clear that the Republican Party in Maryland was almost certain to run someone against him in 1982 based on his leadership role in passing the treaties.

The treaties were finally ratified by the Senate on March 18, 1978, by a 68-32 vote, after months of debate, and with several reservations added during the course of debate. 52 Democrats and 16 Republicans supported them. It is inconceivable that an international issue of this controversial nature would ever be passed with a bipartisan vote in today's US Senate. It was unclear up to the last vote whether the threshold of 2/3's would be reached. Several senators in both parties made courageous decisions to vote "Aye," knowing full well that their votes put them in political peril.

The Chesapeake Bay

In Maryland, unlike Virginia, the Chesapeake Bay is almost sacrosanct and a symbol of the state. That is perhaps because 90% of the state lies within the Bay watershed, whereas that figure is much lower in Virginia. Marylanders have a visceral identification with what is usually described as the largest tidewater estuary in the United States. Of course, much of the commerce on the Eastern Shore and Southern Maryland is dependent on the bay and its tributaries. Crabs are as popular in my hometown in Western Maryland as they are in Annapolis. It is this identification that, over the many years, has led the Maryland congressional delegation to spearhead the bay cleanup effort.

As the Federal Government and its agencies took on more responsibility for restoring the bay, various Maryland elected officials at the state and federal levels accepted the challenge of leading the parade. First and foremost was Senator Charles "Mac" Mathias, the progressive Republican from Frederick. He and several staff members worked diligently for years to pass legislation in Congress that authorized and appropriated funds for new bay initiatives. Mac became "Mr. Chesapeake Bay," and he deserved that title. He was also the senior member of the congressional delegation and thus chaired our mutual efforts with strong bipartisan support from the 10 members (8 House members and 2 U.S. senators).

In 1986, facing the rising tide of the conservative takeover of the Maryland Republican Party and a good chance that he would be unable to win his primary, Mac decided to forego reelection, resulting in the election of Barbara Mikulski, who held the same House seat as Senator Sarbanes. Thus, Senator Sarbanes became chair of the delegation, and I, as senior staffer, became the administrator of our delegation activities. We decided at the outset to make the bay the delegation's top priority. The Maryland delegation was noted for its solidarity and organization. I would prepare the agenda for each meeting, having cleared it with the administrative assistants of the other 9 members. Members would bring delegation letters to our meetings for everyone to sign in support of grant applications from around the state a procedure I believe is unique to Maryland. We became very efficient at procuring funding for a wide variety of programs throughout the state, including the bay.

We had two terrific project directors in our office. First, John Porter, a Naval Academy graduate, came to us without any Hill experience but quickly learned the ropes. The second was Charlie Stek, whom we hired from the office of Congressman Clarence Long, after his retirement. Charlie had been handling bay issues on Long's staff and had been instrumental in several important innovations, such as using the spoil from Baltimore Harbor dredging to build new ecologically sound islands in the estuary. Senator Sarbanes then took on the mantle of "Mr. Chesapeake Bay" as we introduced new legislation and sought additional appropriations from the EPA, the Corps of Engineers, and other agencies responsible for the cleanup effort.

After his retirement from the Senate in 2007, Senator Sarbanes's leadership for the bay has been recognized and applauded. At the University of Maryland Eastern Shore (UMES), there is now the Paul Sarbanes Endowment Fund, which provides "need and merit-based scholarships to undergraduate and graduate students in the environment science program." In 2025, UMES established a coastal ecology teaching and research center at Assateague Island. Overlooking Sinepuxent Bay, the facility is dedicated to the study of inland waterways, with a focus on life in their ecosystems. It is now the Paul Sarbanes Coastal Ecology Center, recognizing "a true champion of the Chesapeake Bay."

Charlie Stek, now retired, has received numerous awards for his leadership and stewardship.

Authorizing Completion of the 103-mile Metrorail System

In 1989, Ron Dellums in the House introduced his bill, HR. 1463 to authorize additional federal funding for the Washington Metrorail system. Sarbanes was the ranking member among the four Maryland and Virginia senators and agreed to spearhead passage of the bill in the Senate. He asked me to organize the effort and serve as the principal contact with both the House delegation and the Senate Commerce Committee, as well as the three regional senators Mikulski, John Warner, and Chuck Robb. I immediately began organizing the group's meetings and developing a strategy to pass the bill. It authorized funding for the completion of the then-planned 103-mile Metrorail system, with its projected total of 83 stations. We worked together as a team. Steny Hoyer played a key role in ensuring that the US Department of Transportation was on board with the concept and would publicly support it. Finally, our efforts succeeded when the bill passed the Senate on October 25, 1990.

The Mini-Filibuster Protecting BWI a Noble Effort but a Lost Cause

The announcement by the US Department of Transportation that it planned to transfer ownership and operation of National and Dulles Airports to an independent authority, the Metropolitan Washington Airports Authority, to be governed by a 17 person board appointed by Virginia, Maryland and the

District of Columbia, set off alarm bells in the Maryland government which owned and operated BWI Airport located between the two metropolitan areas stating that the change in ownership would put Maryland's airport at a distinct disadvantage both in the short and long term. The Governor asked Senator Sarbanes to lead the opposition to the legislation introduced to implement the change. He agreed to do so. After the legislation was reported favorably out of the Senate Commerce Committee over the objections of its chairman, Senator Fritz Hollings of South Carolina, Sarbanes began to filibuster the bill on the floor, with me sitting in a chair beside his desk. Thus began our only filibuster a somewhat comical lost cause from the very beginning.

As I recall, the filibuster lasted about three days. Senator Mathias would spell Sarbanes from time to time, but obviously did not have his heart in it. We were trying to protect Maryland's interests without much detail to support our case. Fritz Hollings, one of the last Dixie Democrats, was noted for his sense of humor and debating ability in his unique southern accent. He was a colorful ally, and I was spending so much time on the floor that we became buddies. When the period of the lease was extended from 35 years to 50 years, an amendment we tacitly supported, Hollings came over to me and said, "Bud, 50 years is a long time. Maybe even Strom Thurmond will be dead by that time."

This futile effort reminded me to a certain extent of the fruitless panoply wars between the Italian hill towns in the early Renaissance period, where the competing armies with their shiny armor, beautifully caparisoned horses and lovely and colorful crocheted cod pieces would sally forth from their villages' perches to confront another opposing city force costumed equally outrageously. Whichever was deemed the prettiest won, and both sides retired to their bastions to crochet larger and more spectacular cod pieces.

**Speaking of cod pieces this is one of
the best Bronzini's "Lodovico Capponi"
at the Frick**

Western Maryland's National Freeway

This road project was one of our top project priorities for many years, the other being the Port of Baltimore. For years, Maryland had wanted to construct, mostly with federal funding, a new interstate highway from Hancock, MD to Morgantown, WV, thus establishing a new and more direct route for traffic from

Baltimore and Washington, DC to Southwest Pennsylvania and the industrial Ohio Valley, an important destination for much of the goods being imported and exported through the port.

One of the major obstacles to construction was Sideling Hill Mountain, a 2070-foot-high ridge dividing the western part of the state. In lieu of building a tunnel, as had been done on the Pennsylvania Turnpike, it was decided to make a dramatic cut through the mountain, replacing the dangerous, curving road of Route 40 over it. I recall that obstacle quite well, since I crossed it many times when Hagerstown High School played Allegheny County's two high school teams. It took many hours to get to Cumberland due to the treacherous mountain road. We worked with the US Department of Transportation and the House and Senate Appropriations Committees for more than 10 years to secure funding for the new interstate. It finally opened to traffic in 1982.

The Sideling Hill cut became famous among geologists and the public for its size and for exposing over 800 feet of previously unseen rock layers, including some obvious coal seams. As part of the project, a rest stop was installed on the side of the mountain with a pedestrian bridge crossing the interstate so travelers going in both directions could access it and its museum featuring the cut's geology.

Commuter Rail

Maryland's Department of Transportation had made commuter rail an important priority early in the senator's tenure, including trains that provided service from Martinsburg, WV, through Western Maryland to Washington, DC, as well as the much more heavily used route between Baltimore and DC. We managed to get additional funding in several transportation appropriations bills for both routes.

An amusing incident occurred while celebrating our success. The senator decided that he and I should ride one of the evening trains to Brunswick in Frederick County while passing out leaflets explaining our role in making the service available to our constituents. We started in the lead car and were making our way to the end car when I ran out of leaflets. The senator was miffed, so I pretended I had more in the first car, went back, picked up the ones we'd already distributed to commuters and managed to give every rider at least a brief glance at our material.

Both routes are now extensively used, and Maryland is now considering expanding its Baltimore route into northern Virginia since so many Marylanders work in that area.

Democratic National Conventions

The senator had agreed to chair the Maryland delegation to two Democratic National Conventions: the first in 1984 in San Francisco and the second in 1992 in New York. He asked me to be the administrator for the delegation, including ensuring their credentials were in order and that the delegates' guests were accommodated. I found this most enjoyable since it allowed me to handle most of my responsibilities in the morning while exploring two of my favorite cities.

The 1984 convention was held at the Moscone Center in San Francisco, with the San Francisco Hilton serving as the Party's headquarters. I stayed with the Virginia delegation at the same hotel I used when headed to Vietnam in 1968. I met with the senator and the delegation each morning to keep them informed and ready for the day. Knowing that I'd traveled extensively around the Bay Area previously, he asked me to provide some suggestions for post-convention travel. I enthusiastically recommended Muir Woods and the Point Reyes National Seashore. I'd written to Governor Mario Cuomo months before, urging him to run, though I recognized it was a long shot. He chose not to, but he gave one of his most memorable speeches at the convention, which I watched on TV while having my afternoon cocktails at the Cliff House along the ocean.

After the convention, I once again traveled north to Point Reyes seeking to enjoy its great beauty all by myself. I was walking up the trail to the seal rocks at the end of the peninsula when suddenly I heard people calling out, "Bud Moss, it's great to see you." Half of the delegation had followed my directions and greeted me: Senator and Christine Sarbanes, Senator Barbara Mikulski, and several House members. Later that evening, I went to my favorite restaurant, which was again filled with friends from the delegation. My reverie was shattered.

In 1992, I was again in charge of the Maryland delegation's arrangements at the convention in New York. Father Kyrill and I stayed in the Bishop's Suite at our favorite boutique gay hotel in the West Village, the Incentra Village House, owned and run by a retired foreign service officer. Many of the rooms were named after the various places he'd served abroad. Stephanski wanted to go on the convention floor one day, so I arranged credentials for him. He sat with the Samoan delegation and was amazed at their size and girth and by a baby the size of a small whale. He loved it.

The day after the convention ended and Clinton was nominated, we were eating breakfast in a Greek corner deli opposite Madison Square Garden when we watched him leave by bus on his now-famous bus tour of America.

Sarbanes-Oxley

This was almost certainly his crowning achievement, and it came long after I'd retired from his staff. Here is Senator Sarbanes' statement on the origin of the legislative initiative: "The Senate Banking Committee undertook a series of hearings on the problems in the markets that had led to a loss of hundreds and hundreds of billions, indeed trillions of dollars in market value. The hearings set out to lay the foundation for legislation. We scheduled 10 hearings over a six-week period, during which we brought in some of the best people in the country to testify ... The hearings produced remarkable consensus on the nature of the problems: inadequate oversight of accountants, lack of auditor independence, weak corporate governance procedures, stock analysts' conflict of interests, inadequate disclosure provisions, and grossly inadequate funding of the Securities and Exchange Commission." The effort was triggered by the massive default and bankruptcy of two corporations Enron and WorldCom. I had a vested interest in the subject because I held almost 1,000 shares of WorldCom, which became instantly worthless.

The Sarbanes staff, as Chair of the Senate Banking, Housing and Urban Affairs Committee, was superb, including Martin Gruenberg, who went on to become Chairman of the Federal Deposit Insurance Corporation, Steve Harris, Pat Malloy, Steve Kroll and finally, for a brief period, Gary Gensler, who is now Chair of the Securities and Exchange Commission.

The new law drafted by the Sarbanes staff imposed strict reporting requirements on corporations and required greater independence and separation between corporate accounting firms and those that employ them. One of the highlights of the law was a provision that allowed the SEC to force a company's CFO or CEO to disgorge any compensation earned within one year of misconduct that results in an earning restatement. Although controversial, the law is now considered an important step toward ensuring corporate accountability.

Former Federal Reserve Chairman Allen Greenspan praised the Sarbanes–Oxley Act in 2005: "I am surprised that the Sarbanes–Oxley Act, so rapidly developed and enacted, has functioned as well as it has ... the act importantly reinforced the principle that shareholders own our corporations and that corporate managers should be working on behalf of shareholders to allocate business resources to their optimum use."

One of the interesting aspects of the passage of Sarbanes-Oxley was the senator's recognition that the legislation faced dim prospects absent bipartisan support. He then began courting a Republican member of the Banking Committee, who, during the hearings on the bill, had shown an interest in seriously addressing the problems the hearings were uncovering. With that senator's support, he was able to put together a coalition to move the bill to the floor of the Senate and to undergird his effort to gain support from his counterpart in the Republican controlled House, Mr. Oxley. This would, of course, be much more difficult or perhaps impossible to pull off in today's US Senate.

The Joint Economic Committee

This, too, is an area where I believe Senator Sarbanes' contributions have never been fully acknowledged. Among Senator Sarbanes' early professional experiences on his return from Oxford was serving in the Kennedy White House as an assistant to Walter Heller, the Chairman of the Council of Economic Advisers. A proponent of Keynesian economics, Heller had a major role in US economic policy under both the Kennedy and Johnson administrations. The Joint Economic Committee (JEC) was founded in 1946 as part of the Employment Act, the groundbreaking law that guided much of our lives after World War II. A joint committee of the House and Senate, whose chairmanship rotates every two years between the two bodies. Senator Sarbanes chaired the JEC in 1987-1988 and again from 1991-1992. We had our own superb staff of economists on the committee.

Sarbanes was fortunate to have, for part of his chairmanship, a partner in economic leadership with his friend, Senator James

Sasser of Tennessee, who chaired the Senate Budget Committee and, after his defeat, served as ambassador to China. They worked together very closely and were both behind-the-scenes advisors to George Mitchell, the Majority Leader.*

*Only once was I called on to chair a fundraiser for Senator Sarbanes and another senator that being Jim Sasser. I put together my only $ 5,000-a-head event with President Clinton as the guest speaker. It was held in the ballroom of the St. Regis Hotel just a few blocks from the White House. I was able to sell lots of tickets, so it was a roaring success for both senators. It was that evening that I had my photo taken with the senator and the president. I was seated at the event with the Sarbanes family. When Sarbanes was introducing the president, he said, "And my mother, Matina, got up early this morning to bake traditional Greek cookies for you, Mr. President." At which point, Mama Sarbanes said in a loud voice to me, "Bud, those cookies aren't for the president. They are for George Stephanopoulos."

In 1991, the two released a joint position paper on the economy entitled "A Program for Recovery and Growth." It was, in reality, a broadside against the unresponsiveness of President George H. W. Bush's administration to the economic situation, which they described as "a country today which faces two distinct economic problems: a short-term problem of recession and a long-term problem of slow income growth and inadequate investment." Their solution was to provide short-term counter-cyclical stimulus and to improve the overall level of investment in the economy and the real incomes of working people. This was to be accomplished through fiscal and monetary policy.

They concluded their report by calling for a shift of substantial resources from the military budget to fund a Marshall Plan for America. "This public investment would be directed at programs that expand our country's capacity to produce and compete in the future including infrastructure, education, research and development and worker training." In rereading this paper recently, I realized how sound their advice was then and is still today. If only we would follow it once again.

Despite these many accomplishments in his 30 years in the Senate, I have always felt that he could have achieved so much more. As his academic record attests, he was a brilliant man who could easily have forged a path in the House and the Senate to rival that of Senators Phil Hart or Ted Kennedy. He was extraordinarily and needlessly cautious. He was never ever in any political peril. He was popular to the point that he won most of his elections by about 60% of the vote. I always thought these results would have buoyed his confidence and enabled him to become a more active legislative advocate. In the end, I realized that it was not in his nature to be what I wanted him to become. I still admire him greatly; however, knowing his potential, it was very frustrating over my 18 years in his service to see that potential unfulfilled.

Chapter 22
Death of Mother

Mom and Ira sold our farm and the two office buildings Dad had bought in Hagerstown after renting the commercial buildings and the apartments above them for many years. Ira did a great job in maintaining the properties and taking care of the tenants. They eventually bought a small one-story, three-bedroom house in the northern part of Hagerstown. Throughout the 1970's, they continued to live active lives, including taking cruises and trips. On one such trip, they traveled first class on the SS America to Italy and were seated at the same table as Joseph Hirschorn and his wife.

As my mother and stepfather (Ira was 11 years older than mom) had grown weaker, Phil and I had moved them to a Lutheran-run senior center in Williamsport, near Hagerstown. It was very difficult for both of them, especially Ira, who was used to his independence and mobility. Mom was very unhappy there despite the excellent care she was receiving. She died on September 17, 1985, at the age of 77. She had cleverly invested Dad's money and left Phil and me a considerable inheritance. I was the executor of her estate, which was made much easier by my having placed her assets in a living trust with a local bank. Ira lived for several more years at the same home where he was one of the few men and became very popular with the women.

My mother was, in many ways, the inspiration for my life in almost all its aspects. She was highly intelligent, strong-willed, organized, determined and sensitive. There were times, I believe, when she became frustrated by fulfilling the traditional role of a wife and mother, while recognizing that her ability transcended that of her male contemporaries. I posit that she enjoyed sex very much since one weekend when I came home, Ira pulled me aside and said that my mother was feeding him aphrodisiacs. He then told me in his usual matter-of-fact way, pointing to his crotch, "that thing stops working all on its own." I think Dad adored her, although there were rumors that he strayed from the garden path from time to time. My Aunt Mary (dad's only sister) and my brother both concluded that mother had a decided preference for me, which may have influenced Phil's being so different from me in being gregarious and outgoing. I believe they were probably correct in their analysis, although I was completely oblivious to it at the time. My friends in Washington who knew her adored her.

I'm afraid I have rather neglected our father, Benjamin Franklin Moss. Not intentionally, I believe, but more due to the overwhelming influence of our strong-willed mother. Dad was a great success in life despite his wretched upbringing in rural Washington County, having been raised in poverty, provided little education and then, while still a child, subjected to divorce, family feuds, a stepmother and God only knows what else. His natural grace and enthusiasm for life masked, I believe, a constant struggle to overcome that background. He was a born salesman and quickly established one of the most successful independent insurance agencies in Western Maryland. He was a loving husband and father, and I only wish he'd lived longer so that we could have known and loved each other as mature adults.

My parents were amazing. Of all my friends in Hagerstown when I was growing up, mom and dad were the only ones who had taken the extraordinary step of sending their young sons abroad for the summer to live in another country. I believe they knew that, in doing so, they were launching Phil and me into worlds neither of us had ever experienced or imagined, with the possibility that the trip would open new horizons and new insights for both of us into the world outside Hagerstown, Maryland.

Chapter 23

Dinner at the Harriman's

In the late 1980's, Pamela Harriman, wife of Governor Averill Harriman, became active in national Democratic politics. She very quickly formed a political action committee and hired staff to assist her. Typically, she used Averill's vast resources to forego establishing an office in a commercial property. She simply bought the historic house next door to theirs on N Street in Georgetown and opened it as her new headquarters. Pamela Harriman had led a life that would make most mortals blush. She was married multiple times, including to Randolph Churchill, Winston's son, Broadway producer Leland Hayward and finally Harriman. In between were multiple lovers, including Stavros Niarchos. As one wag described her, "…she has become a world expert on rich men's bedroom ceilings."

As part of her outreach to Democrats, she began courting Capitol Hill staffers, including the most senior chiefs of staff to U.S. senators, which, of course, included me. About 8 of us received an invitation to dine at the mansion on N Street. We had our cocktails in the terraced garden, followed by a formal dinner in their elegant dining room, where small Monet landscapes covered the walls. Her domestic staff was entirely English and could have doubled as downstairs staff in Downton Abbey. They made you feel inferior for not knowing which fork to use. After dinner, we retired to the spacious library for dessert and after-dinner drinks. I was seated next to Governor Harriman at a sofa end table, looking for a place to set my drink down. I had to choose between moving either a Fabergé imperial Easter egg or a gold cigarette case, a gift from Bobby Kennedy. I moved the cigarette case.

Later in the evening, I needed to use the loo, so I approached one of the incredibly snooty butlers and asked where I might find it. His response was, "Go to the end of the library and turn right at the Van Gogh." Needless to say, the evening is etched in my mind mostly because of being in the presence of such an amazing couple, who, oddly enough, came across as rather ordinary. President Clinton later appointed Pamela as ambassador to France, where she served with distinction for 4 years. The Van Gogh "Sunflowers" now resides in the National Gallery.

Chapter 24
Retirement 1994-2001

In 1991, I'd bought my historic 1829 country house, Glen Burnie, in Fluvanna County, Virginia, and had decided to make it my retirement home, although that hadn't been my initial reason for buying it. Senator Sarbanes was up for re-election in 1994. In almost all his previous elections, I'd been the principal fundraiser for his campaigns, meaning that, to do so legally, I had to go off the Senate payroll and be paid by the campaign frequently for periods of up to six months. I told him, as we approached the 1994 campaign, that I intended to retire in 1995 after his successful re-election to a 4th term. He was not happy about that but accepted it as a given.

After buying Glen Burnie, I sold my apartment 201 at Crescent Place, where I'd been president of the co-op board for many years. Our friends and neighbors, Alan Gilbert and his wife, Nimet Monasterly, allowed us to stay in their apartment 202 for about 5 months while they were in France taking care of her mother. I later leased apartment 205 until I retired. Thus, I wound up being the only resident of the co-op to have lived in three different grand apartments. Apartment 201 was one of the largest co-op apartments in Washington, with almost 2,700 square feet, including a living room, dining room, library, owner's suite with bath, bedroom and study, and guest suite with bedroom and bath, plus a butler's pantry, kitchen, and servant's room with full bath. It was glorious. The living room was huge some 30 by 25 feet. Here is a photo of my living room before I moved in.

Living Room, Apartment 201, 1661 Crescent Pl NW

While residing in 201, I was elected president of the Crescent Place Board of Directors, a position that required close attention not only to the shareholders but also to the maintenance and operation of the building. I was also very active in the neighborhood, including frequent meetings with Ambassador Walter Cutler, the President of Meridian House International, which was located across the street from our building. Residents were a colorful lot, including Edith Kermit Roosevelt, granddaughter of Teddy Roosevelt, and several retired ambassadors. My final temporary home before moving to Glen Burnie was with my friend, Chandra Hardy, at her lovely home.

We lived quietly together for about 5 months. I came home, had a glass of wine (or two) with her and played Schubert on the creaky piano while she read some enormous tome on the economy of Fiji (or somewhere). She has now reposed. I was a great admirer of Chandra and miss her.

Stephanski had returned to Washington to complete his master's degree in sacred theology and begin work toward his PhD at Catholic University, so he was fortunately back living with me in the apartment. This was a period of bliss for both of us, although he was a most serious student and I was still running a large senate office. We hosted many visitors during this period, including local friends, foreign visitors, the Sarbanes staff, and our interns. Leaving apartment 201 was a difficult decision since we'd spent six happy years there in a stunning apartment which lent itself to entertainment and sybaritic enjoyment.

I decided to end my Senate career by hosting a joyful sendoff in the US Senate Caucus Room, with guests invited not just from Capitol Hill but also from high school and West Point, friends, family, colleagues from all over Maryland, my ski buddies, and so many others. There were more than 250 in attendance, and it was truly festive.

Senator Sarbanes Paying Tribute at
My Retirement Party 1995

Mama Sarbanes, Christine & Michel Sarbanes and
Senator Mikulski in her Pretty New Dress
She Bought just for the Occasion

During my retirement festivities, Stephanski, I and our wonderful Italian friend, Lou Ventino (aka Luigi) were staying at Chandra Hardy's classy abode. Luigi, who'd graduated first in his class at Johnson & Wales in Providence, RI, and thus got to travel to Paris with Julia Child, offered to cook us a gourmet dinner. It was a spectacular success with a different wine with each course. Chandra was so happy that she was lying on the floor after dessert, saying, "If only I'd married three gay men!"

Chapter 25

Ditchley Foundation

Over many years, I'd become a close friend with Congressman John Brademas of Indiana through his Greek connection with Senator Sarbanes. They were also both among the first Greek-American Rhodes Scholars. He'd served as the Majority Whip of the House for several years, after which he became President of New York University. At the same time, I'd met Ambassador Phil Kaiser, one of my all-time favorite friends and characters. Son of a large Jewish family from Brooklyn, he graduated from the University of Wisconsin and was one of the first Jewish Rhodes Scholars specializing in labor law at Balliol. He served as Assistant Secretary of Labor in the Truman administration and later as principal advisor to Governor Averill Harriman. He then served in four important diplomatic posts as ambassador to Mauritania, Senegal, Hungary and Austria. One of his sons, Robert, became managing editor of the Washington Post. Another, Charles, is gay and lives in New York and wrote the definitive history of early gay life in that city. Phil and I frequently had lunch together and found great pleasure in each other's company.

I had lunch with Phil just before my retirement. During lunch, he told me he was one of the American directors of the Ditchley Foundation, an Anglo-American foundation dedicated to increasing understanding between our two nations and our allies. He invited me to the next Ditchley Conference to be held in June. Ditchley is a stunning 18th-century English country house near Oxford in the center of an immense agricultural estate. It hosted Churchill during much of the Second World War since it was safer than Chequers.

Ditchley House Saloon with Trophies dating to 1610

I was also invited by John Brademas, who chaired the American Ditchley Foundation. I readily agreed, although the subject was one I knew little about, which, oddly enough, is one of the strengths of the foundation. The philosopher, Isaiah Berlin, an early supporter of Ditchley who had a strong influence on Ditchley's approach, wrote a letter that still guides it in framing meetings, advising that it was important to include "all kinds of apparently irrelevant persons," dreading otherwise "a lot of dull-faced men probably saying it had all been very interesting..." He stressed the value of leaving space for informal conversations and urged against too many presentations. I was quite happy to consider myself one of the "irrelevant persons."

The conference was titled "Corruption in democratic societies patterns, implications and remedies." There were participants from Britain, Canada, Egypt, Germany, India, Japan, Mexico, Spain and the US. Brademas chaired the conference, and Phil was one of the conferees. I'd made a less-than-sterling start to my Ditchley stay by wandering through its gardens and coming upon a lady removing goldfish from a pond. I asked her how long she'd been a gardener there, and she responded, "I'm not the gardener. I'm Lady Wills, and I own this place." I bowed or curtsied respectfully.

The first evening, there was a black-tie cocktail party in the great hall, followed by dinner in the immense dining room (70 people seated at one table, with liveried footmen attending us). England was that weekend under a hot spell for which they are congenitally ill-prepared. At the dinner (men in black tie and ladies in formal gowns), it was stiflingly hot, abetted by dozens of blazing candelabras on the table. I asked if we could open some of the windows, only to be told they were permanently sealed, so no one could pilfer the two Van Dyke paintings at the ends of the room. We fled to the garden as soon as dinner was over.

I was selected to serve on a subgroup asked to delve into the question of governmental philosophy and approaches to corruption. I was seated next to a man I came to admire greatly Sir Simon Jenkins. He was an author at the time and later became the managing editor of The Times of London and president of England's National Trust, the wonderful organization that spearheads the preservation of the nation's historic and natural sites. He and I quickly hit it off and decided to propose a then rather radical idea that democratic governments had a duty to train their civil servants in the importance of integrity and the observance of national and international law regarding corruption, including education in those areas. In the later plenary sessions, we carried the day by having our ideas adopted in the final report. After the conference, I took the train to London with Phil, his wife and Brademas.

Chapter 26

Life in Retirement

When I retired, I was quite secure financially with my new federal pension, my substantial savings from my mother's legacy, and the rent from my Capitol Hill townhouse. That was not my concern. My chief worry was that since I was only 57 when I retired, I wanted to continue my life of stimulating work and enthusiastic participation in my community especially my new home in Palmyra, Virginia. I must admit that I was unsure how Father Kyrill and I, a gay couple, would be received in this very conservative traditional community.

Stephanski had been a strong advocate of buying Glen Burnie, including its restoration. We'd hired a Charlottesville architect to work with us on planning and executing the house's restoration. Before that, we'd been coming down almost every other weekend to clear the weed trees and the invasive vines from the meadow and the boxwoods in the garden. It was heavy work, but we were enjoying it. We sometimes stayed on futons on the third floor of the house but later started checking into the Fork Union Motor Lodge in that town, where we always had the same room, far from the traffic on Route 15. We'd produced immense piles of debris, and on several occasions almost burned down Fluvanna County. We then became a bit more cautious.

Our plans for the house, which had been abandoned for 18 years, were to restore the principal floor to its 1829 configuration including the removal of a powder room in the back hall, update all the utilities, plaster the walls, remove the 1950's drop ceiling in the great room, install modern appliances in the kitchen, and finally once that was all done to set about scrapping dozens of layers of paint away from the historic woodwork and either refinishing it or repainting it. This project started in 1994 after we finalized the plans. We also installed a bath off the great room, new closets, and a dumbwaiter that served all three floors of the house. We hired a Charlottesville contractor who started out well but, many months later, walked off the job, prompting us to mediate with them over their existing contract and their work. This was all happening while I was still at work in the Senate a difficult situation not helped by our somewhat inattentive architect. We came out of the mediation owing about $20,000 to the contractor, far less than the $80,000 they had been demanding. We had to hire a new contractor, Skip McCormick, a skilled carpenter who did a great job completing the restoration.

We finally moved to Glen Burnie in August 1995 after my official retirement. In 1999, I hired an architectural historian to prepare the paperwork for my application to place the restored Glen Burnie on both the Virginia Landmarks Register and the National Register of Historic Places at the Department of the Interior. Both were approved, laying the basis for my later decision to place the house and its acreage under a very restrictive historic easement with the Virginia Department of Historic Resources, which took effect in 2001. Now, Glen Burnie is protected from development in perpetuity, including under any subsequent owners, since the easement must convey with the deed.

One idea I had was to organize a series of lectures on international relations and domestic politics. I, of course, had many contacts, and my honoraria contracts started coming in. I gave a well-publicized lecture, entitled "American Democracy at the End of the American Century," at Salisbury State University on Maryland's Eastern Shore. Later, I presented the same lecture at Ball State University in Muncie, Indiana, hosted by my Greek friend, Professor John Koumilides. The Maryland State Teachers Association asked me to give two talks on Maryland's changing political demographics, as did the Democratic Caucuses of the Maryland General Assembly. I was invited to join a panel on the 1996 presidential election at the Naval Academy. Later, while in residence at Annapolis, I was asked to assist professors in classes on both domestic politics and foreign affairs, which I very much enjoyed.

In 1996, I continued my political fundraising by being hired by Mark Warner to raise money for the Virginia Democratic Coordinated Campaign as part of his initial effort to be elected to the US Senate, funds to be used by all the Democratic candidates on the ballot that year. Mark knew me from my work in Washington and still knows me as Bud. I raised over $250,000 for that campaign by working from an office in West Richmond and from home. Since Mark had guaranteed a substantial sum for this campaign from his personal fortune, he was quite grateful for my success in reducing his exposure. Much of the money came from my longstanding friends in the labor unions. That was followed by my six-month stint at the Naval Academy, discussed below.

I'd, of course, stayed in close contact with Senator Sarbanes, and in early 1999, he asked me to chair his finance committee for his 2000 re-election campaign, with the understanding that I would do most of my work from my home, with trips to DC for specific events and fundraisers. I agreed to do so only if he was willing to pay me a substantial monthly fee, since I was already deeply involved in many local projects and would have to spend time away from them to fulfill my responsibilities. I was pleasantly surprised that many of my old friends in the labor and business communities, as well as individuals, were so forthcoming. Needless to say, it was a great success, although I was exhausted in the end. In 2002, his son, John Sarbanes, hired me as his deputy campaign fundraiser, and I again brought in about $50,000 for his first congressional campaign.

Chapter 27
National Historic Public and Records Commission

I became aware of the work of the National Historical Publications and Records Commission (NHPRC) at the National Archives when the US Senate appointed Senator Sarbanes in the early 1980's to fill its statutory position on the commission. The NHPRC was created by Congress in order to assist the Archives in preserving America's historic records in all forms. It is the only grant-making component of the Archives and includes two representatives of the executive branch appointed by the President, a member from the judicial branch, a US senator, a member of the House of Representatives, the historians of the Defense Department and State Department, as well as participants appointed by national historical and archival associations. Its statutory chair is the Archivist of the United States. Due to my long-standing interest in history, I chose to attend all its meetings, whether or not Senator Sarbanes was present.

It very quickly became obvious to me that the commission's work was both very important and little appreciated. When Sarbanes was unable to attend due to Senate business, I sat in his place and, after a number of years, was accepted as almost a fully participating nonvoting member. I reviewed hundreds of grant requests and advised the senator on which to fund. Among the interesting members were Justice Harry Blackmun, who represented the judicial branch, and Al Goldberg, who had been the Defense Department historian for decades and was a colorful, occasionally dissenting voice. The Archivist was the former Democratic governor of Kansas, John Carlin.

When I decided to retire in the summer of 1995, I asked Senators Sarbanes and Mikulski and Congressman Steny Hoyer to recommend me to President Clinton for the vacant executive branch position. They sent glowing letters to the White House, and I was told that Senator Mikulski called the personnel office and told them that I was her top priority. I received my first presidential appointment on November 10, 1995, soon after my retirement. The commission usually met at least 2 times a year. I became deeply involved in its work in a short time and enjoyed it immensely. Soon thereafter, Senator Sarbanes was replaced by Senator Mark Hatfield of Oregon, so I was probably one of the few on the commission to realize the irony that the author of Roe vs. Wade (Blackmun) was then seated opposite Hatfield, the principal author of legislation to overturn Roe.

Some of the quandaries and challenges facing the NHPRC were the increasing reliance of public officials on email and electronic communications and the question of how to preserve those records and the continuing outlay of the commission's shrinking appropriation for the documentary editions of the Founding Fathers, many of which had been in the works for decades. In 1999, Justice Blackmun was replaced by Justice David

Souter. Since he and I represented two major branches of government, we were always seated together. It took several meetings for him to warm up to me. He is a very reserved man; however, that side of his personality hides a wicked sense of humor, which I only discovered later. Soon after his appointment, the commission elected me to chair its newly created Executive Committee, which was meant to advise it on its short- and long-term goals and priorities. I became very active in organizing the committee, which usually met several days before our regular business meetings.

Soon after Justice Souter joined the commission, the Archives was undergoing restoration, so he invited us to hold our meeting at the Supreme Court. He gave all of us a personal tour of the entire complex, culminating in the small, unpretentious room where the nine justices meet in conference. It was there that he told this remarkable story. Soon after the fall of the Soviet Union, a lawyer friend of his from New Hampshire asked David if he would give a tour of the court to his Russian friend, an expert on US judicial history and proceedings. David agreed. When in the conference room, David asked the Russian what he thought the most important decision made at the table was, thinking he would say Brown v. Board of Education, which was exactly what the rest of us were thinking. The Russian then said to David, "No, the most important decision made at this table was Nixon vs. the US. Do you know how important that decision was to a man raised under the Soviet system to have your nation's leader declared subject to the laws of the land like any other citizen?" David was astounded and agreed with him.

In 2000, with the election of George Bush, I realized that I could be replaced on the NHPRC, although I'd been reappointed to another full four-year term by Clinton before he left office. The commission traditionally gathered for lunch in the spacious office of the Archivist, which I loved due to its wonderful portrait of FDR behind his desk. David usually joined me for lunch. This time, he was seated at the other side of the room when I realized that many members were gathered around him. I went over and listened. David was lamenting the Supreme Court's decision in Gore vs. Bush, calling it one of the worst decisions the court had ever made. I was surprised that he, a man of few words who almost never spoke publicly about the court, was doing so and in the presence of many historians.

NHPRC 2000 Marvin & David Souter in Center Back Row
Archivist of the US, John Carlin, in the middle of the front row

President Bush replaced me on the commission in 2002, so I reluctantly bid farewell to an organization I both cherished and to which I'd made important contributions. Justice Souter, when he received word of my removal, wrote me in his own hand the following letter, which is one of my most cherished possessions.

Supreme Court of the United States

July 22, 2002

Dear Bud.

I'll greatly miss crossing paths with you at the NHPRC twice a year.

Your very good sense and very good will have made my own time on the Commission happier and more satisfying than it would have been without you, and less mystifying, too, thanks to your understanding of what was going on.

Not every historian down the line will realize his professional indebtedness to you, but your friends on the Commission always will.

Justice David H. Souter

Chapter 28

US Naval Academy

Perhaps one of the most surprising and unusual activities in light of the Army's perpetual rivalry with it was to become the staff director of the largest and most important study of the Naval Academy in its modern history.

How did this come about? The Senate had again appointed Senator Sarbanes to serve as a member of Annapolis' Board of Visitors, a body created by statute to advise the academy and review its operations regularly. It consists of members of the House and Senate as well as presidential appointees. As a consequence, I'd been attending Board meetings for over 13 years and had become fascinated by the institution while also being concerned about some of its operations. In 1995-1996, the academy experienced a series of jolting scandals, including cheating and, perhaps most peculiar of all, a ring of midshipmen who stole and sold cars. To address these problems, the Navy recalled Admiral Chuck Larson, Supreme Commander Pacific, to serve as superintendent and address serious morale and other issues at the academy. I had worked with him during his previous tenure as superintendent, some years earlier, when he was a two-star admiral, so he knew me quite well. He was a very fine leader at that time, and I admired him and his work.

One of the strangest and funniest meetings of the Board occurred in the late 1980's. President Reagan had appointed a used car salesman from Texas to the Board a loud, rather preposterous man. His other appointee was the columnist George Will a real contrast between the two. At the meeting, Senator Sarbanes was late, and I was sitting in his place when the car salesman, who was now the chair, began berating the then-superintendent for his handling of a controversial case involving a midshipman athlete. He disagreed with the punishment and offered a resolution overturning the superintendent's actions, which was obviously illegal under the Board's statute, since its purpose is simply advisory and it has no role in the day-to-day governance of the academy. George Will was clearly unaware of the law and sat silently. I then saw the senator's driver walk in. I ran out, cornered the senator, told him about the Texas cowboy's resolution and explained quickly its illegal nature. He walked in, claimed the floor and gave a five-minute Harvard Law dissertation refuting the Texan's resolution. The other Rhodes Scholar, George Will, chimed in on our side at that point, Oxford colleagues to the end. We carried the day.

In late 1996, I learned that the Board of Visitors, to lend gravitas to the effort to ferret out the causes of the academy's serious problems, was about to appoint a stellar group of military and civilian leaders to a Special Committee under its control. In learning over the years about Annapolis and its operations, I'd become increasingly concerned that the Navy was not providing the academy with the best and brightest officers for its academic and military programs, unlike West Point, where an assignment there is much coveted and is frequently an essential step toward the higher ranks. In light of this, I called Senator Sarbanes and made a simple request. I wanted to testify to the Special Committee to voice my concerns. Unbeknownst to me, he took that as a signal that I wanted to be involved in a full-time position with the study, so he communicated that to Senator Mikulski, Congressman Steny Hoyer and Congresswoman Beverly Byron, who was a recent presidential appointee to the Board. They contacted both the superintendent and Admiral Stan Turner, who was then a member of the Board. I was completely unaware of any of this.

I was scheduled to give a lecture on Maryland's future political demographics to the Democrats in the Maryland House and Senate in early January 1997. Just before I left, I received a call from Admiral Larson's aide de camp asking me to meet him in his office after my talk. So, I spoke at the State House and trundled over to the academy. Admiral Larson and his deputy took me into his office and announced that they wanted me to become the executive director of the Special Committee, to relocate to Annapolis for 6-7 months, to live in an admiral's quarters in the BOQ and to head a staff of three other highly qualified assistants. I was flabbergasted. I told him that this was a surprise and that I would obviously have to discuss it with my family before I accepted. I drove back home, and the fathers immediately insisted that I take the position, and so I did.

The next six months were among the most intense and difficult in my life. I had a superb staff assigned to me (with one exception). The members of the Special Committee were a daunting group. They Included:

Co-chairs

Dr. Judy Mohraz, President of Goucher College

Admiral Stansfield Turner, former Director of the CIA and Commander in Chief NATO's Southern Command and Mediterranean Fleet

Ambassador Richard Armitage, former Assistant Secretary of Defense and later Deputy Secretary of State

Congresswoman Beverly Byron, wife of my former boss

Commander Tina D'Ercole, one of the first women to graduate from USNA

Brigadier General Thomas Draude, USMC (Ret)

General John Galvin, Dean, Fletcher School of Diplomacy, Tufts University, and former Supreme Allied Commander Europe (USMA 1954)

Holly Hemphill, Principal, Groom and Nordberg law firm

General Robert Herres, USAF (Ret), Former Vice Chairman of the Joint Chiefs of Staff

Father Theodore Hesburgh, President Emeritus, University of Notre Dame

Ronnie Liebowitz, Principal of Hellring Lindeman Goldstein & Siegel law firm

Senator John McCain

Frederick McClure, former White House assistant to President Bush for Legislative Affairs

Rear Admiral Benjamin Montoya USN (Ret) Chairman Board of Visitors

Dr. Steven Muller, President Emeritus, Johns Hopkins University

Admiral Paul Reason, Commander in Chief US Atlantic Fleet

Kevin Sharer, President of Amgen and a USNA graduate

Vice Admiral Richard Truly USN, (Ret), Director of the National Renewable Energy Laboratory, Golden, CO

Jack Watson, Jr., Former White House Chief of Staff to President Jimmy Carter

Larry Werner, Partner and Director of Ketchum Public Relations

Although I knew Admiral Turner and Dr. Mohraz only by reputation, I got to know both relatively quickly through a series of meetings at the academy and later at Admiral Turner's home in McLean. They were highly motivated people whose goal was clearly to do the best job possible for the future of the academy and its central role in the Navy. They pretty much gave me free rein until, in the end, Stan Turner vetoed some of my proposals, which were the very reasons I'd gotten involved with the Special Committee to begin with. That was my only disappointment.

It was obvious to me that Admiral Larson and his staff respected me and recognized that I had strong support outside the academy community, including the Maryland congressional delegation. It was two months or so in my work when it was announced that Secretary of State Madeline Albright was going to be addressing the Brigade of Midshipmen. I decided to go and was dressed very casually when I went to the arena. I had known Madeline for some years, since she visited our office fairly frequently in her various positions, as Sarbanes was a ranking member of the Foreign Relations Committee. I also knew her chief of staff, Ambassador Wendy Sherman (Wendy was, until recently, Under Secretary of State in the Biden Administration), who had been Mikulski's chief of staff in the House and Elaine Shocas, a Greek friend who was Assistant Secretary for Legislative Affairs. After the speech, I wandered over to say hello. The whole gang saw me and called out loudly, "Bud Moss, what are you doing here?" They then invited me to join them at the formal reception, where we spent much time talking and enjoying each other's company. Meanwhile, Admiral Larson and staff were observing all of this closely.

All of this became somewhat relevant when I was forced to go to Larson's chief of staff, Captain Henry Sanford, to complain about the staff member they'd assigned to me, who was not, in my estimation, carrying out his assignments well. I was very forceful with Captain Sanford and threatened him something I would not have ordinarily done; however, I was very angry about the unfairness of my excellent staff working together and being paid while their colleague was slacking off. I said, "As you saw the other evening, if I have to bring the battleship Missouri up the Severn to train its guns on your office, I'll not hesitate to do so and will have loads of support from my friends in Washington." That argument carried the day and led to improved relations with my staff assistant.

My favorite member of the Select Committee was General Jack Galvin, Supreme Allied Commander Europe (NATO) during the fall of the Berlin Wall. He came from Tufts frequently and wanted to be heavily involved in meeting with faculty, midshipmen and staff. I very much enjoyed setting these up and sat in on all of them. I carefully arranged it so that a panel of young Naval officers would outline how they came to teach at Annapolis and how, in doing so, they found that their careers were not being enhanced. Jack Galvin, who had taught at West Point, was shocked. He was ultimately very disappointed when my effort to include this fact in our final report was vetoed by Admiral Turner, who was reluctant to take on the whole Navy establishment on this question.

I had another rather interesting confrontation with Admiral Larson near the end of my tenure. My staff and I had met with the superintendents of West Point and the Air Force Academy during their annual conference in Annapolis. Lt. Gen. Daniel Christman from West Point outlined for us the changes in curriculum and training (including new majors) being implemented there. I tried to include some of those initiatives in our report, suggesting that majors in international relations and foreign languages be emphasized and given priority. Larson protested. I then went to meet with him to make a last-minute effort to change his mind. As we were talking, I noticed that on the shelves behind his desk were the various hats, awards and decorations bestowed on him as CINC Pacific in his travels in his command ship. Finally, in desperation, I said to him, "Admiral, arrayed behind you is the evidence that you spent much of your time as CINC PAC in a quasi-diplomatic role. That is precisely why I am trying to change your curriculum to make those skills more available to your graduates." Despite my best efforts, this was ignored in the final report as well.

Most disappointing on the committee was Senator McCain. The only meeting he attended was the kickoff, and he never set foot in his alma mater after that, nor did he have staff participate or seek clarification on the issues we were exploring. I was aghast in the end when he objected to some of our findings in the final report without any basis for doing so.

The report we published in June 1997, entitled "The Higher Standard Assessing the United States Naval Academy," was the most thorough and complete study of the academy in modern times. Much of it was later implemented by the Navy command structure. Several committee members and I were invited to present the report to Secretary of the Navy, John Dalton, in his Pentagon office after lunch in his private dining room. The photo of that event is below.

Secretary of the Navy John Dalton Thanking Me
for Leading the Study Effort

Chapter 29
Capitol Square Preservation Council

Having known Mark Warner for many years, I enthusiastically joined his campaign for governor of Virginia in 2001. Throughout our many years of working together on various political campaigns including his 1996 US Senate race, he was fully aware of my keen interest in historic preservation and my work with the Fluvanna Historical Society. After his successful election, he then in 2002 appointed me to the Capital Square Preservation Council, the body responsible for the building and grounds of Virginia's historic capital. I was quite excited to take on this responsibility since it was a personal priority, and I was a great admirer of the building, the core of which was designed by Thomas Jefferson.

We met frequently in the Capital. The staff was first rate, and the members of the council, including the senior staff of the Virginia Senate and the House of Delegates as well as the appointed members, were all committed to maintaining the architectural and historic fabric of one of the most important such complexes in the United States.

It was during this time that the state had decided it needed to expand its office space in and around the Capital and for the first time to construct an appropriate visitors' center with emphasis on the building's historical importance. We also were, of course, responsible for overseeing the development and maintenance of the historic grounds surrounding it and the governor's nearby residence.

The plan submitted by the state authorities was one that gave me much pause. It included tunnelling under the grounds, installing the new museum and visitor's center in a building there as well as additional rooms for the elected officials and staff. I was very much opposed to this plan since I felt that the public access to this magnificent building should not be through a subterranean tunnel but through the attractive grounds. I suggested that the state purchase one of the attractive abandoned buildings on Broad Street, make that the visitor's center and provide shuttle buses to the grounds. Mine was a distinctly lonely position. I voted against it, but it was approved almost unanimously with the exception of an architect friend of mine on the Council who joined me in my opposition.

I thoroughly enjoyed my six years on the Council and was very active in all its deliberations and work. I only wish that my concept had been more actively and completely explored before the final decision was made.

Chapter 30

Paul Danqua

Although I met Paul quite by accident (or perhaps not), I became fascinated by him, his enormous talent and his scintillating ability to entertain, to challenge and to speak the Queen's English in a manner that left one almost speechless. Being in his presence reminded me of a passage from Edith Wharton's memoir where she was seated next to a man she'd never met before. Here is her description: "Within five minutes, I was whirled away on such a quick current of talk as I had not dipped into for many a day. He moved with dazzling agility from topic to topic, tossing them to and fro like glittering glass balls." The first evening I met him was in the 1980's, when he was serving as the World Bank's publicist, an important position he took quite seriously. My friends, Martin and Chandra Hardy, then owned and lived in the Laughlin Phillips mansion on Foxhall Road, Washington's most exclusive address. Phillips was the son of Duncan and Marjorie Phillips, the founders of America's first museum of modern art. Martin is English, a Cambridge graduate and was an economist at the International Monetary Fund. Chandra, who recently died, was from a large Asian Indian family in Guyana, held degrees from the London School of Economics, was a senior economist at the World Bank, and was a friend of Paul. They'd invited me to dinner and, I believe, seated me quite deliberately next to Paul.

Paul Danqua was the son of one of Ghana's early political leaders who was defeated for the presidency by Kwame Nkrumah. He was instrumental in founding the University of Ghana and its affiliation with London's University College. Paul's mother was an Englishwoman named Bertha May Walcott, and he was given the name Joseph Walcott at birth. He changed his name to his fathers at an early age. His life partner was Peter Pollock, sole heir to a large Midlands industrial fortune. Paul was an actor, TV personality and solicitor, among many other things. He starred in the breakout 1960's movie, A Taste of Honey, playing the role of the Black sailor who seduces Rita Tushingham. She won the Cannes award that year for best actress in that role.

While he and Peter were living in Battersea, they invited the young British painter Francis Bacon to share their flat. Bacon was giving them his sketches in lieu of rent, and they were simply storing them in a suitcase. It was only in the 1990's, after Bacon had become one of England's most famous painters, that they opened the suitcase. They notified the Tate, which acquired them in 1996, and mounted a major exhibition at the museum in 1999 to unveil them.

The very distinguished Paul Danqua in his law office

That night, Paul and I had a conversation on every conceivable topic, including my travels and experiences in Africa and our preferences in classical music and in plays. I could tell as the evening wore on that he was becoming enamored with me, finding me perhaps a bit more sophisticated than he'd originally surmised. At the end of the dinner, he tapped his glass to get everyone's attention and then announced, "I now realize that I was deliberately seated next to Marvin this evening, and during the brief period we have been together, I have fallen madly in love with him. I, therefore, propose that he accompany me in my Rolls-Royce to the Wheaton Plaza Shopping Center (the world's tackiest), where I will seduce him." I was utterly delighted at the prospect, but alas, it was not to be. His Rolls-Royce was indeed parked outside.

The second dinner with him was equally entertaining. Again, we were seated together. The conversation headed toward English drama, winding up with a discussion of which of Oscar Wilde's plays I preferred. I, of course, said "The Importance of Being Earnest." Again, at the end of the dinner, he rang his glass and called for silence. He then proceeded to act out the entire last act of Earnest from memory in character, including placing his napkin over his head while playing Miss Pringle. It was a marvel to behold. I was delighted.

A few weeks later, Stephanski and I were at the Kennedy Center for a concert by the London Symphony Orchestra. At intermission, we were headed for the bar when Paul Danqua, wearing a gorgeous full-length purple African robe, swept across the vast open space. He shouted a greeting, calling me "his darling Marvin." Stephanski had heard my tales about him and knew who he was. He then invited both of us to join him and his friends from the orchestra for cocktails in the rooftop bar, saying, "After all, I have banged the entire percussion section of the orchestra." We joined them and had a wonderful time. Later, Stephanski said to me, "How is it that you meet the strangest people in the world and they fall in love with you?" I had no ready response to that question.

My last evening with him before he and Peter moved to Tangier was again at the Hardys'. He'd brought his large extended family from Ghana all his half-brothers and sisters (I think about 6, as I recall). During dinner, he told me he'd brought them to England and America to teach them the Queen's English and how to dine properly. They were obviously enchanted with this strange, exotic relative and loved him deeply. It was beautiful to see. That was the last I ever saw him, much to my regret. He and Peter moved to Tangier, where Peter opened a restaurant that became the social center of Tangier's large expat and gay communities. Peter died in 2001, and Paul in 2005, both at the age of 90. They are buried side by side in Tangier. I was blessed to have known this enchanting, remarkable man, if only fleetingly. **Requiescat in Pace**.

Chapter 31
Active Retirement

To say that my retirement years from 1995 to the present have been among the most exciting and productive in my life may sound odd in light of what I've written in this saga about my previous travels and experiences; however, there is much truth in that. I was unsure how we (Father Kyrill and I) would fit into the relatively conservative rural society of Fluvanna County. In many ways, the direction of my retirement life was a result of something I had absolutely no control over - the unanticipated and unparalleled enormous and sudden increase in the county's population. From 1995 to 2008, Fluvanna was the second-fastest-growing jurisdiction in Virginia, eclipsed only by Loudoun County in the DC suburbs. When I'd purchased Glen Burnie in 1991, the population was about 12,000. It is now almost 28,000, and although the rate of growth has slowed remarkably, it is still growing.

How did this fact act as a catalyst for my involvement in community affairs? It became apparent to me almost immediately that the county was struggling to deal with the challenges of rapid growth. With my strong interest in history, I'd become an active member of the Fluvanna Historical Society, a dynamic and well-run organization led by a remarkable woman, Ellen Miyagawa. The county had taken a controversial step in 1994 by paying $1 million for a large historic estate, Pleasant Grove, just south of the Rivanna River, to build a new courthouse and other government buildings. Another nascent community organization was then founded to take advantage of the almost 1,000 acres of Pleasant Grove, to include building a trail system, and I became a charter member of the Fluvanna Heritage Trail Foundation. It was during this time that I was restoring Glen Burnie, placing it on the National Register of Historic Places and putting it under easement. I saw that my example was a good one for conserving open space amid rapid population growth. I also realized I could begin using my knowledge of federal and state grant programs to help the county address some of the more dire consequences of the recent changes.

One must bear in mind that during this period, I was also lecturing, fundraising for politics, leading the study at the Naval Academy, and serving on the NHPRC. I was a busy man. I'd also gotten involved with the local Democratic Party and was soon serving as vice chair. In talking to other like-minded folks in the county, I began thinking that one potential threat was the possible loss of farmland, forests, and open space. Having been involved in the senate with programs on Maryland's Eastern Shore and Southern Maryland that brought citizens together to discuss their heritage and form organizations to protect their communities, I raised the idea of holding a series of heritage forums on the subject. I also started working with Ellen Miyagawa and the Historical Society Board to broaden the Society's mission to include viewscapes and land preservation, shifting away from a singular focus on historic buildings.

In 1998, I applied on behalf of the Historical Society for a $25,000 grant from the National Park Service to begin organizing and holding a series of heritage forums. The grant paid for hiring Tanya Denckla (Cobb) from UVA's Institute of Environmental Negotiations as our forum coordinator. We worked with dozens of local citizen groups and non-profits to ensure that the public was fully involved in the process. The initial forum, entitled "Fluvanna, Our Heritage, Our Future, Our Decision," was held on March 26, 1999, at Camp Friendship, with almost 300 people in attendance, including representatives of all our state and federal elected officials. It was a great success and laid the groundwork for preserving, protecting and promoting the county's natural and cultural heritage.

It is difficult to capture the impact I've had on my adopted county. It has been profound. I think the best way to document it is to simply list the major projects I spearheaded and helped finance as President of the Fluvanna Historical Society and the Fluvanna Heritage Trail Foundation. They include:

- Design and construction of the Village Park in Palmyra
- Chairing the committee working with VDOT to design the award -winning Route 15 replacement bridge in Palmyra
- Instrumental in hiring a county grants administrator and, with her, wrote the first successful transportation enhancement grant. It provided for the construction of the Village Park, stabilization of the historic Palmyra mill on the Rivanna and design and construction of the ADA accessible Sandy Beach Trail at Pleasant Grove

- Converted the Heritage Trail organization into a public non-profit, which then became a partner with Fluvanna County on many of its initiatives

- Grants for the design and construction of the picnic shelters at Pleasant Grove. They were designed by Carlton Abbott, one of Virginia's leading landscape architects

- Served on the Board of Supervisors for 5 years and chaired it for 2 years, including the period when we financed the design and construction of our new high school, one of the most modern and beautiful in the Commonwealth

- Partnered with the county in applying for and receiving over $750,000 in public and private funding for the restoration of the Pleasant Grove House and its summer kitchen. The project received Preservation Piedmont's award for best restoration that year

- Led the effort to fund, design and build the award-winning Palmyra Fire Station, including my own design for the southern façade.

- Assisted in raising almost $300,000 for the design and construction of the Fluvanna Farm Heritage Museum at Pleasant Grove

- Personally designed the solar demonstration building at the library and provided its funding through grants

- As president of the Historical Society, spearheaded the successful effort to place thousands of acres of Fluvanna's open space under conservation or historic easements

- Led the effort to purchase the CSX rail right-of-way in Palmyra and to convert it into a rail trail

- As president of the Historical Society, worked with a local foundation to target funding for the purchase and restoration of Maggie's House for the headquarters of the Society, to restore the Holland-Page Place log cabin museum and to create an endowment for the maintenance of those properties

- Served on the committee to design and build Fluvanna's spacious new public library and led the effort to heat and cool it using a geothermal system

- Chaired the initial meeting of the newly created Rivanna River Basin Commission and later served as Chair, Vice Chair and citizen member on that organization

- Chaired the Environmental Task Force in 1999-2000 in preparation for rewriting the county's Comprehensive Plan. Now serving on the Rural Preservation Committee for the latest update

- Gave talks and lectures on public-private partnerships in Virginia and Maryland, many sponsored by the National Park Service

Chapter 32

A Day with Prince Charles

After we converted to Holy Orthodoxy, I became a member of the Friends of Mount Athos, an Anglo-American-Hellenic organization organized some 30 years ago to support the monasteries on the Holy Mountain in Greece. The Royal Patron of the Friends was Prince Philip, and his deputy was Prince Charles. The membership was virtually a "who's who" of Orthodox studies worldwide. I would note that Prince Philip's mother, Princess Alice, became an Orthodox nun and is buried at the Russian convent on the Mount of Olives in Jerusalem. I was one of the few members without an OBE, a royal title, or any other distinguishing notation after my name. In 2002, the organization arranged to hold its annual meeting at Highgrove, Prince Charles' home in the Cotswolds, so I eagerly signed up (unfortunately, I signed up rather late, so I was unable to get permission for Father Kyrill to attend with me).

Most people, including most English, are unaware of Prince Charles' longstanding interest in Orthodoxy. On several occasions, Prince Charles went on a private pilgrimage to Mt. Athos, staying at the great and venerable monastery of Vadopedi, the same monastery where Father Mefodii was a monk in 2000. Prince Charles was in residence on one of his stays while Father

Mefodii was there. He assiduously followed the rules for visitors, including attending all the services.

Father Kyrill and I flew to England and stayed several days in London. We went to visit St. Paul's Cathedral and were walking around when an Anglican priest, seeing Father Kyrill in his vestments, approached us and introduced himself. He was Father Duncan, an Indian, who served parishes in East London. After a brief conversation, he led both of us behind the ropes around the high altar and asked Father Kyrill to chant the beginning of our Orthodox services; thus, we were there, under that vast dome, singing and praising God. I had tears in my eyes. We then visited some of my favorite gardens on the way to Tetbury, the town near Highgrove. I arrived at Highgrove at 10 am, went through security at the gate and was greeted by the leaders of the Friends.

At 11 am, Prince Charles arrived and opened the program with a talk I will never forget. I was taking notes while he was speaking. He was obviously aware that his audience was different from many he'd addressed before, so he began in a way that was most unexpected (I think the fact that there was no press present was a relief to him). He said his stays at Vatopedi had influenced his thinking, including the desire to eradicate egocentrism and to celebrate a sense of the sacred. One of my favorite quotes from the speech was "I abhor the fact that people are terrified of being odd or different." He went on to decry the modern penchant for "remaking man for our own purposes." He stated that his role in life was "in the face of paucity of spirit, to dedicate his life to restoring from disintegration the values of society." He closed by saying something dear to my heart, "that what we build is a physical expression of the values we hold." His last statement was "The only places where I feel completely at home are at Vatopedi and here at Highgrove. Highgrove is not a royal residence. It is mine, and I am creating not only beautiful gardens but a form of farming that is organic and sustainable." I felt like standing and cheering.

After the program, we had a short interlude with wine and canapes before lunch. During that time, Prince Charles and I talked for about 15 minutes about diverse subjects, including historic preservation, gardening, and Orthodoxy. I mentioned that I'd visited his much-vaunted new town, Poundbury, and he asked me what I thought. I was very candid, saying that I loved the idea but found the execution somewhat sterile and wanting. He seemed to agree. In the last minutes of our conversation, I asked him if he'd ever visited his grandmother's grave in Jerusalem. He said that he had not since he was prevented from going to the Holy Land for security reasons. He then asked me to say a prayer for him at her grave when I am next in Jerusalem (as if I went there all the time). I came away a great fan, realizing how very different he was from the then-public image of a cold, calculating man in light of the death of Diana. I found just the opposite.

Prince Charles & Marvin Highgrove — June 2002

He started our tour of his amazing gardens and then turned it over to one of his gardeners. He has done a splendid job in a short period, creating an imaginative garden with distinct design concepts from one to another. He, of course, had the assistance of some of England's leading gardeners, including Rosemary Verey, who designed his borders and Miriam Rothschild, who provided the seeds for his wildflower meadow. Deep in the garden is his small chapel, designed like a miniature Byzantine church. He told the amusing story of purchasing an enormous olive oil vat in Spain, about 15 feet tall and shipping it to the Prince of Wales in Tetbury. The owner of the Prince of Wales pub in Tetbury was surprised when they tried to deliver it to him. He simply said,

"Wrong Prince of Wales." Father Kyrill and I went on to Wales, which we loved, including Bodnant Garden, one of my favorites.

Chapter 33

Breakfast Club

Some years ago (I really don't remember when), my friend Robert Bryan invited me several times to be his guest at a discussion group that meets biweekly in Charlottesville, composed of many distinguished gentlemen from the area. Over 50 years ago, Brigadier General Harry Disston, a resident of Albemarle County and a noted equestrian, had an inspiration. He wished to form a new gathering of gentlemen for comradeship and enlightened discourse. It was to be a small group with a rather specific purpose operating in a structured setting. It is called The Wednesday Breakfast Club.

It consists now of up to 12 members. The structure is really quite simple. There is a brief social gathering followed by breakfast. Discussion is then led by a host, one of the members, who lays out a subject for discussion, making sure the issue is not known to his colleagues in advance. A 60-minute discussion of the selected topic then ensues. The Club has had many members over its 57 years, including active and retired professors, generals, politicians, attorneys, and businessmen. When a member resigns or reposes, the group selects a replacement. After several visits, I was asked to join and have enjoyed being an active member ever since.

After reviewing the archives of the group and the biographies of its diverse membership, I decided in 2014 to compile and write the club's history. It was a challenge because some of the bios of the original members were missing, so I had to undertake research to find out who they were. My original history was published in 2016, and I've now prepared an addendum to bring it up to date. The discussions cover a vast area and are always stimulating, interesting and frequently on subjects far afield from some of our own expertise, which was, after all, General Disston's original purpose. Every time I am to be a host, I have threatened to make my subject erotic Persian poetry. I think some have been disappointed that I've not followed through on my promise. In addition, some of the members have become close friends and were among those urging me to write this rambling story of my unusual life.

Chapter 34

Unsung Hero Award

Each year, the Virginia, Maryland, and Delaware Electric Cooperatives give a single award to a Virginia citizen who has been a leader in community service. Unbeknownst to me, my friend, Judy Mickelson, nominated me for this award with a strong letter of support from Senator Paul Sarbanes, who, incidentally, was always a strong supporter of the New Deal cooperative movement. Judy was notified that I'd been selected and asked me to accompany her to Richmond in February 2016 to witness her receiving an award. In reality, it was I who was to be honored. I agreed. However, nature intervened that weekend with a massive snowstorm, so the event had to be cancelled. Of course, Senator Sarbanes did not get the word, and he called me to inquire when the award would be given. I, of course, had no clue what he was talking about, but he let the cat out of the bag. I telephoned Judy to thank her for nominating me and told her how ironic it was that a US Senator had blown her cover. Which reminds me of an apt quote from Charles Lamb: "The greatest pleasure I know is to do a good action by stealth and have it found out by accident."

I was honored by the cooperatives at a ceremony held in March 2016 at our historic courthouse, which was filled with many Fluvanna friends, guests from elsewhere, and members of the Breakfast Club. The citation they gave me reads in part: "For embodying throughout his life, and pursuing through his daily actions, a devotion to and passion for serving others, as a soldier, as chief of staff to a US Senator, and for the past 20 years as a tireless volunteer and community leader in Fluvanna County, Virginia. And serving as a golden example of what volunteerism is all about, helping others without thought of, or desire for, personal gain or recognition, the Electric Cooperatives of Virginia, Maryland, and Delaware bestow their 2016 Unsung Virginian Award on Marvin F. Moss."

Award Presentation

This award, in many ways, summarized my contributions to Fluvanna County. When I first moved to Fluvanna permanently in 1995, I was casting about, trying to find my niche in an entirely new setting. In doing so, I wound up not only becoming engaged in almost every aspect of life here but also leading the efforts of two non-profits, the Fluvanna Historical Society and the Fluvanna Heritage Trail Foundation. I served on the Board of Supervisors for 5 years and chaired it for two. I brought with me a vision of what Fluvanna could become, and through years of concentrated effort, I believe I've transformed it into a more attractive and vibrant place. I have always loved Christopher Wren's epitaph on his tomb at St. Paul's Cathedral in London: "If you seek my monument, look around." I realize this sounds terribly hubristic; however, I think it is, in reality, an understatement. I am still surprised today that I have been able to accomplish so much in my community, and I am happy that public recognition of those achievements might inspire others to follow in my footsteps.

Chapter 35

Julann Griffin

I've tried many times to recall when and how I first met Julann. It is lost in the mists of times past. However, that may have occurred, it has been a sheer delight for me to have her as a friend for so many years. She is now 95, and despite the toll that age entails, she is still a vibrant, loving, charming, kind and invariably funny person. Despite her marriage to Merv Griffin and her many famous Hollywood friends, she is the salt of the earth, and you can only extract tales of these folks from her with difficulty. I'd heard about her from a mutual friend who'd served as a waiter at a party she had at Chatham, her beautiful historic home, where the guests included Mel Brooks and Anne Bancroft. Dom DeLuise, Alan and Arlene Alda, Carl and Estelle Reiner and Gene Wilder. I've enjoyed her company countless times and have come to admire her even more as she took care of her younger sister, Maureen, who died while living with Julann.

Julann in her garden still surprised by the world

Born and raised in Michigan, she still has that Midwestern manner of candid, forthright expression. Although Merv was responsible for bringing Jeopardy to fruition on national television, the idea for the game was Julann's, hatched on a plane, where she outlined to Merv the simple idea of giving an answer to a question and asking panelists to provide the question. Even at this late stage in her life, she and her niece, Candy, are still inventing new games to be marketed to internet audiences.

Julann articulated to me many years ago her theory about Fluvanna County and the many eccentrics who've settled here. She believes there is a force out there causing this to happen, something inexplicable but real. She, of course, includes me and many of my friends in the eccentric category. She played minor roles in two of Gene Wilder's now-forgotten films: The Haunted Honeymoon and The Woman in Red. Evidently, the last film is so bad that it has become a cult favorite. She tells the story of Merv and her effort at the beginning of their television careers to hire a comedy writer. After advertising in New York, they selected a stunning winner, Mel Brooks.

At a dinner just before Christmas some years ago, Stephanski and I barged in on her unannounced. She and her guests were already at the table in her elegant dining room. She welcomed us (she actually seemed relieved that we were there) and introduced us to her two guests. One was Princess Cecilia de Medici, Duchess of Tuscany, and the other was a handsome young Portuguese count, Carlo, who was her amanuensis. The evening went off the rails almost immediately when she announced that she was a fascist and had been whisked away from her apartment at the Pitti Palace in Florence by the Mafia after the Red Guards threatened her life. Stephanski, once again, was clearly wondering how Marvin had once again dragged him into a world of total insanity and unreality, but by this time, he was fairly used to it. Later, she proudly announced that her family, the Medicis, had invented love, war and the fork. The fork brought tears of laughter to Stephanski, who by this time, was actually enjoying himself. I had dinner once more with Cecilia at Julann's and again at the home of other Fluvanna friends. And so, Julann's theory was borne out once again, as Cecilia was then living in Fluvanna County.

Chapter 36
Glen Burnie Gardens

My brother, Phil's, cartoon satirizing my fascination with daffodils

We began planning Glen Burnie's gardens almost immediately after buying it in 1991. As I studied the land there, I realized that the bones of a natural garden were already present with daffodils blooming on the meadow and forest verges as early as February. These daffodils, which were evidently brought from England centuries ago, are the English forest daffodil, narcissus pseudonarcissus. The meadow lent itself to the planting of even more bulbs. Other potential sites were the one-acre pond below the house and the shaded intermittent stream that flowed into it. I also viewed the large earthen dam as a stage for planting below it. We spent the first years there on weekends clearing invasive trees, vines, and other monstrosities from the meadow and the woods. We also began dividing and transplanting daffodils, a process that is still underway today.

The concept of the garden evolved over time, but early on I decided that the key to success would be recognizing the nature of the rolling terrain around the house and the presence of a sizeable water feature. These features would assist me in making the garden appear natural, however contrived it actually was.

One of the important elements in the early plantings was my long-standing friendship with David Dethero, a friend from my service in Ethiopia. David, after leaving the Army, was trained as a forester and naturalist, ultimately purchasing land high in the mountains outside Flat Rock, NC. He had learned how to propagate native American azaleas and rhododendron and was collecting seeds from the balds of the nearby Great Smokies. He ultimately founded his own nursery, Hurricane Gap, specializing in these unusual plants, and was one of the few to do so successfully. He provided dozens of plants for my early plantings, many of which quite miraculously still survive.

I'll simply mention each of the major gardens here and illustrate them with several photos.

Meadow

The Stream Garden

The Pond Garden

The White Garden

The gardens at Glen Burnie are an ongoing project. Here it is 2023, and my gardening team is still planting trees, dividing and transplanting daffodils, weeding beds, and helping to remediate the enormous damage from the January 2022 ice and snowstorm. Gardens are never finished, and it is my fondest hope that the next owners of this magical place will understand and appreciate what they've inherited.

My gardens were begun and conceived at a time of hopefulness, a time when we, as a people and as a nation remained confident that we could face the challenges of a changing climate and a society increasingly fragmented, with a consequent loss of commitment to universal community standards. They are now maturing in a period of anxiety, retreat and accusation. It is, therefore, an uncommon pleasure to walk each morning through my gardens and to think perhaps naively that life will someday return to normal.

Chapter 37
Marvin the Dabbler

As my friends know, I've always been fascinated by classical music and the fine arts. I don't pretend to be an expert in either, although I've spent some considerable time studying both. I had piano lessons starting at the age of six and can still pick out a Schubert sonata on my 1910 Duysen grand piano, although the Fathers, who usually run to their quarters when I start playing, once said to a guest, "Marvin plays all the notes but not necessarily in the order in which they were written." Not exactly a vote of confidence.

I came in second place in the nation in the National Scholastic Arts Contest when I was in the 8th grade, having produced a lovely ceramic plate in a Pennsylvania Dutch style, using the sgraffito technique to apply the design through a covering slip. I received a $25 treasury bond as a result and was written up in the local newspaper. I've been drawing, sketching and painting in watercolor and pastel in recent years with mixed results. I return to these plunges into art episodically. Sometimes, the results are pleasing, and other times, my lack of training is readily apparent. Nevertheless, I venture to illustrate some in very different mediums for your viewing.

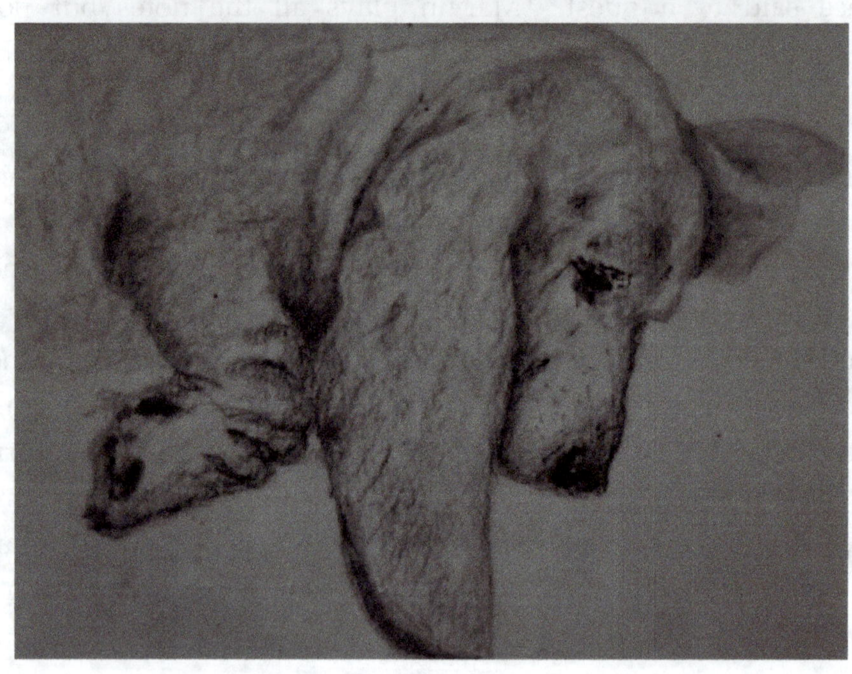

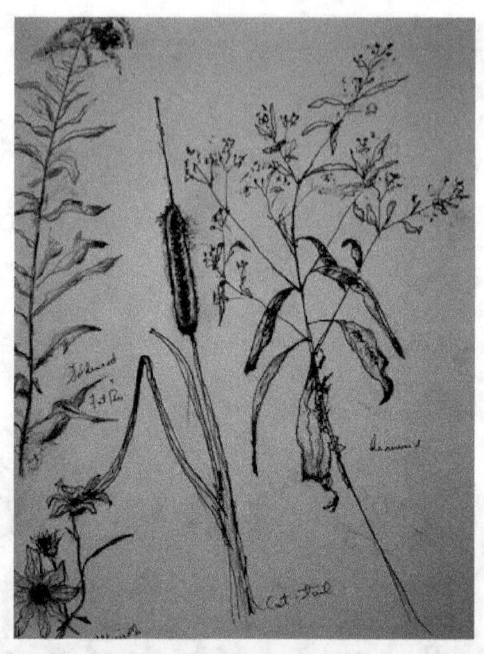

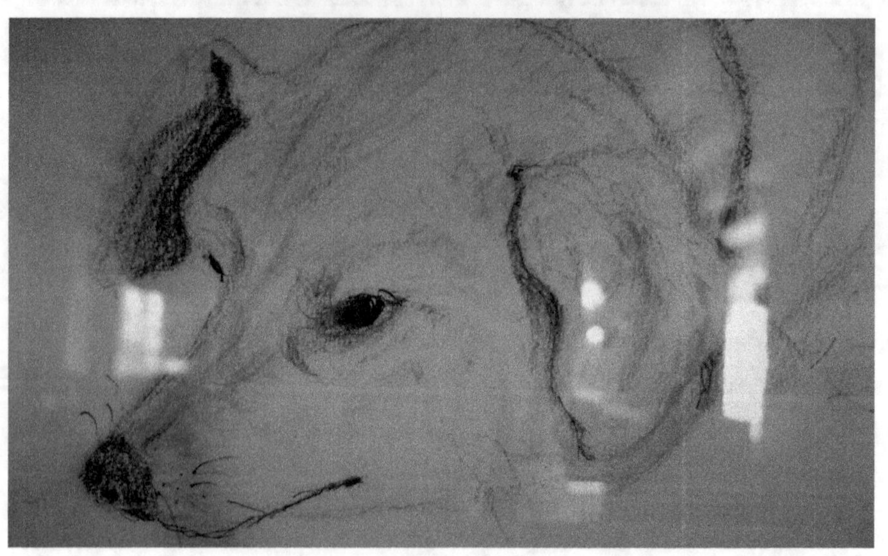

Oops! This is Olimpio Fusco
By John Singer Sargeant

Chapter 38
Father Kyrill and Holy Orthodoxy

I've saved these two subjects for last, partially because it is so difficult for me to write about them. I know that some view me as a man with a complex background, given excessively to pleasure and to lightness of spirit. I also know that I have, many times, fostered such an impression, either deliberately or otherwise. That reputation is, of course, belied by what I've achieved over the past 86 years God has given me. I have been very blessed in my life, and I continue to be surprised each day that I am still alive and able to continue contributing to my family, my friends, and my community.

The Road to Damascus

Our Road to Damascus was a rocky, tenuous and contorted one. It is therefore difficult for me to summarize, but I will give it a shot. After his ordination to the priesthood, when Stephanski was finding life in his Ukrainian Byzantine Catholic parishes early on difficult for a number of reasons, including the indifference or hostility of the rectors where he was initially assigned, I found our conversations filled with his sadness and anxiety. St. Matthew's Catholic Cathedral was just some 12 blocks away from my house on Rhode Island Avenue, and on Sunday mornings, I began walking there to say prayers for him. That soon became a habit, and eventually I attended mass there regularly, although I'd not gone through any of the regular instruction expected of a convert. I then considered myself Catholic - a far cry from my Lutheran upbringing and my long period of agnosticism. I was influenced by knowing and loving Stephanski and by learning to respect his devotion to his church.

Later, when we would be together, he taught me the Eastern Liturgy and how to chant it. We began celebrating Liturgy together wherever we were in our apartment and at Glen Burnie. We converted one of the upstairs bedrooms into a chapel and used the icons Father Mefodii had written to create a small iconostas. After Father Mefodii joined us in 1996, we began seriously thinking of converting to Orthodoxy. The fathers had been heading in that direction for most of their lives, even when they were not consciously aware of it.

We first joined the most obvious of the various national Orthodox organizations in the United States (we, in reality, abhor the idea of national churches since, to our minds, there is only one Orthodox Church) The Ukrainian Orthodox Church, headed by Archbishop Anthony. We were relieved that they celebrated Liturgy and Holy Days using the Julian, or old, calendar. They also accepted the fathers into the church without ordaining them. Then, Archbishop Anthony began allowing new parishes to celebrate on the Gregorian calendar, so we decided it was best to seek a new home. We appealed to the Russian Orthodox Church Outside of Russia, with its headquarters in New York City.

I realize that these distinctions may seem trivial to people unaware of the theology and history of Holy Orthodoxy, but to

Father Mefodii and Father Kyrill, they were of paramount importance. The Russian Orthodox Church Outside of Russia was appropriately named. It was the Russian church in exile after the Communist Revolution. They were first located in Serbia and later in Paris. The New York Archdiocese is located in an enormous mansion on Park Avenue and 91st Street.

Meanwhile, we were attending Liturgy at the ROCOR church in the valley, where the fathers were viewed with some suspicion. I think that was due to their incredible theological education and the seven degrees they held between them. Perhaps, there was also a note of jealousy. The hierarchs decided that both needed to be ordained as Orthodox priests. Father Mefodii (then Father Basil) was ordained first. On a visit to New York, Bishop Gabriel out of the blue announced that both were to be sent to the Holy Land to protect a ROCOR parish in Jericho, a shocking, unanticipated decision. They then spent three months there, both at the women's monastery on the Mount of Olives and in other places. While there, they were befriended by Sister Stephanopoulos, George's Orthodox nun sister. When ROCOR announced it was reuniting with the Patriarch of Moscow, my two Ukrainian priests could not countenance such a decision, so we went off again searching for a new home.

We are now a monastery in the Bulgarian Orthodox Church with Metropolitan Joseph of New York as our North American hierarch. He welcomed us warmly and has been a consistently kind and generous spiritual leader. We have had a small but intensely loyal group of parishioners who travel great distances to participate in the Divine Liturgy. Father Kyrill is confessor to a series of Romanians and Bulgarians who frequently come to the Skete and must believe we are starving, since they always bring tons of food for us.

Father Mefodii had started studying iconography in the style of Saint Andrei Lublev many years ago. His teacher was the Russian iconographer Vladislav Andreyev, born in Russia and trained in traditional methods there. In the States, he founded the Prosopon School of Iconology, which organized workshops across the US and abroad. Father Mefodii excelled and was selected as one of its instructors. He has subsequently held icon workshops in England, Canada, the Philippines, and many cities in this country. He now has his own studio here at Glen Burnie, with students coming from all over Virginia on a regular basis.

We are now faced with the unwelcome reality of both fathers suffering from Parkinson's and the grim possibility that we will be unable to continue the full spiritual life of the monastery.

And now no longer Stephanski but Father Kyrill

Throughout this long tale, I've alluded to my love for Steve, Stephanski, and Father Kyrill, to give him all the names I've delightfully called him for almost 50 years. We met in 1974. It took several years for us to realize that we loved each other and that no matter what happened, we would remain partners. It has not been easy for either of us with our separations and the changes in our relationship over the years through his intense commitment to his faith. And now his suffering from the dreadful Parkinson's

Disease. He spoke of that faith the very first night I met him, and I took it seriously immediately.

I suppose I could best sum up my feelings by simply telling you that each morning when I see him walking from the Skete to the house, he brings a smile to my face and lifts my spirits. When he and Father Mefodii were tonsured as monks in 2001, I knew that our love would be tried once more. But we realized it and swore to each other that our love would endure under these new, totally different circumstances. We then exchanged these letters, which I have never before revealed to anyone. They express eloquently what we felt then and still do to this day.

February 4, 2001

My Dear Stephanski,

In a few days, you will enter a new life reborn in Christ and leave behind those things irrelevant to that rebirth. I have been thinking about what I could give you that would enrich your new life without distracting you (there will be enough distractions). So, I thought to compose this simple letter, which I hope says what our lives together have meant to both of us.

There is no way I can express the joy you have brought to my life over these last 26+ years. All I have to do is look at you, and my heart skips a beat. It is probably immodest and inappropriate to say that we were blessed to have met and doubly blessed to sustain our love and enrich each other in doing so. You have said from time to time that I "saved your life." You did not save my life, but you changed it forever in directions I could never have anticipated. My life is fuller, richer and more complete because of you. The egocentric, occasionally obnoxious and inconsiderate agnostic is, I hope and pray, long gone. Through you, my life has become a new life as well.

Now, you (and I) begin a new life together and apart. We will always be together in spirit and in agape. There will be times when the struggle of sustaining the new Orthodox monastic life will seem unbearable. There will be times when you will be overcome with loneliness, sorrow, self-pity and regret. And then you must pick yourself up and go on. That is what Orthodox monasticism requires of you -- to find what the will of God is and pursue it diligently. It is what I, unworthy layman, would wish for you as well.

I do not think of this new life as one of separation. I think of it as perhaps the inevitable consequence of the conversation we had the first day I met you. You talked that day about things I found simply incomprehensible. I knew then, if we became friends, that in the end there would be something more important to you (and thus to us) and that my role would be to ensure you had the fortitude to follow that road. God has blessed us abundantly, and me specifically, in helping you do that.

And so, I end by saying that you have transformed my life. As long as God grants us time and memory, I will cherish you.

All my love,

Marvin

My dear Marvin,

Why is it that when I begin to write, I burst into tears? A new life in Christ, leaving behind all that is irrelevant? The Lord's love is so demanding. Yes, if this is what the Lord is asking. But, my dear Marvin, you are my life; you are not, and never will be, irrelevant in this new life in the Lord. How could you not be an integral part of my life after these 26 plus wonderful years? You have been the only human being who has loved me so unconditionally, certainly more than I have loved you. If the mere thought of separation is so very painful, how much more will be the reality? You are everything to me, even more than my own flesh and blood.

I am so frightened about this new life and its demands. Will I be able to keep these promises? Will this future find you slowly disappearing from my life? And me out of yours? Will our love grow cold and distant? It was my fondest hope that we would spend the rest of our lives helping each other grow together in Christ. Now, again to go apart? What is the Lord asking of me? Is this the only way to disappear into God?

Growing up in the Lord can be so very painful. Gold is gotten only through fire!

You are right, Marvin. We will be together in a new and better? manner. But I want you to know that I so much love just being around you, seeing your face, hearing the sound of your words and laughter, walking arm in arm, feeling the joy that permeates from your very being, absorbing the confidence you exude, gaining strength from yours, basking in your love. You make me so happy! I am so grateful to Almighty God for His gift of sending you into my life. You have become so much a part of my life; I cannot even begin to comprehend life without you. I do not want to be apart from you ever again!

What I am about to undertake is by far the most difficult thing I have ever done. I must be honest with you, Marvin. I want to do this, and I do not want to do it! If it is the Holy Will of God and it appears to be, whether I like it or not, want it or not then I will humble and beg for His Grace to accept whatever He asks and trust in His ever-loving providence and care for us, His unworthy servants. The tears, however, will still flow, and the ache will still burn, but the love will still grow between us because Christ's love and His Holy Spirit will be our consolation and comfort.

I love you beyond words and measure. More than "deep and abiding!" I love no human person more than you! I am always cognizant of your love for me. I am wrapped in it. And it makes me warm in heart for it fills me with immeasurable joy!

All my love,

Stephanski

You will always be "my Marvin," my only love. May we walk together arm in arm to that glorious Place where we find Love Itself!

Although these letters are sad in that they reflect the end of one form of love, they are, in reality, extraordinarily positive statements of affirmation and commitment to quite another. That is how I view them now and when they were written.

Perhaps this photo says it all. In 1999, we hosted a catered black-tie dinner at Glen Burnie to celebrate our 25 years together with a total of 25 guests.

Chapter 39
Death of Father Kyrill

My beloved life partner, Stephen James Juli, reposed at the age of 77 on January 1, 2026, at the University of Virginia Hospital in Charlottesville, Virginia, due to his Parkinson's Disease. Although he'd been diagnosed 14 years earlier, his death was still a great shock to me and his identical twin, Father Mefodii.

We buried him in a new grave on the grounds of Glen Burnie next to the Skete of St. Maximos the Confessor, where I and Father Mefodii, will also be laid to rest. He insisted we buy Glen Burnie, worked for years to make it more beautiful, and, in the end, led to the creation of an Orthodox presence in an area where none had existed before. Those attending his burial included many who regularly came to him for confession and recent converts who'd just gotten to know him.

I simply cannot imagine what my life would have been like without him. As I indicated in my letter to him in 2001 when he became a monk, he changed my life making me more sensitive to others and finally and most importantly bringing me and host of others to Holy Orthodoxy. He was a modest man, who despite his diffidence, exuded unbounded love for those who entered his world. How blessed we both were to share our lives together.

He'd been exposed constantly to Agent Orange while serving as an enlisted Marine with the First Marine Division in 1968-1969 in Vietnam. We, and the Veterans Administration (VA), believe his Parkinson's Disease was a direct result of that exposure; thus, he was declared to be 100% disabled and eligible for considerable benefits. The VA has done a terrific job over the past 6 years or so in providing home care, his medications, and other assistance, for which we are very grateful. His death occurred at the very time that the Trump administration was firing thousands of VA workers and reducing outreach and administration of its many programs serving our veteran population.

He was the great love I'd always thought and feared I would never find. We were doubly blessed to share our love for each other.

Eternal Memory! Rest in Peace, dear Stephanski!

Chapter 40

A Futile Attempt to Explain it All

Perhaps here is the perfect place in this sometimes amusing, frequently fraught and fitfully serious monologue to attempt a conclusion. But how to go about that? Should my conclusions be about me, about the world I've encountered or a combination of both? Since so many of my friends who encouraged me to write this story and gave me ideas and suggestions along the way wanted it to be a combination, I agree that is the best way to convey the massive changes that have taken place and relate them to my own life.

One could easily conclude that what began in upbeat innocence and naivety has, in fact, ended in a coarser, increasingly frightening, and negative ending. There is a great deal of truth in that, but it is only part of the story.

The American electorate in November 2024 is facing a choice between a reckless madman and a president who is the oldest man ever to serve as president and has achieved much for which he has been given little credit. Such an election between two elderly and controversial men defies the image this country has cherished almost from its beginning as a young, dynamic, stable nation, unlike any other in the world. It also speaks loudly to the rest of the world as a harbinger of future decline and increasing unreliability in the one nation on which much of their own security, both economic and military, is inevitably dependent.

It is important to remember the remarkable litany of successes post-World War II. The US had played a crucial role in turning the tide in that war, developed the polo vaccine, built the then world's largest auto industry, created the computer, launched the jet age, landed astronauts on the moon, pioneered mass high school and college education and forged the world's then largest middle class all in 25 years. There are dozens of books that seek to explore and explain how we have gone from those incredibly productive post-war years to a society riven with doubt, unsure of its foundations, untrusting of its government and traditional institutions, and increasingly susceptible to believing misinformation and deliberate lies.

I believe David Leonhardt's "Ours Was the Shining Dream: The Story of the American Dream" does the best job of detailing the basis for this dramatic transition. As Leonhardt points out, understanding how this has happened is perhaps the best guide to seeking solutions. His text clearly shows that the greatest progress was made possible in the 60's and early 70's by a combination of national elected officials and corporate and labor leaders who shared a common approach to what he calls "economic democracy." With the rise of the Chicago School of economics and its embrace by national business organizations and major corporations, that dynamic began to fade in the late 70's, with its demise secured with the election of Ronald Reagan in 1982.

The intellectual force behind much of this was Robert Bork, aided and abetted by the now-famous memo from future Supreme Court Justice Lewis Powell to the Chamber of Commerce. It laid out a path to take advantage of governmental opportunities to shift economic assumptions to those of the Chicago School, culminating in a clarion call for conservative economists to assist in electing presidents who would implement the memo, including the appointment of justices to the Supreme Court who reflected the new paradigm. They have succeeded probably beyond their wildest expectations.

How one rectifies this is a mystery to me since doing so would almost certainly entail addressing the serious deficiencies in our Constitution. The demographics of the country have changed such that increasingly states with small populations are able to control much of what happens, or more likely does not happen, in Washington. We have now gone for the longest period in our history without a new constitutional amendment, and the likelihood of one now is close to zero, given the composition of Congress and the increasing Republican domination of state governments.

On the other hand, I have witnessed changes in our society and in our legal rights that have had an overwhelmingly positive impact on many citizens, including me. Those changes include the civil rights laws and Great Society programs of the Johnson Administration, the increasing participation of women in our workforce and elected bodies, and a gradual increase in the wage base for most of our workers. And finally, of course, the Supreme Court decisions making gay marriages legal and the ability of gay women and men to serve openly in our armed forces. First among these in my mind is the ending of the Jim Crow era and the legal protections for Black voters. This struggle continues, but I believe that young Americans, with their strongly held views on diversity and inclusion, will help break down the remaining barriers. However, many of these changes also fueled disenchantment among voters who were not thriving in the new economic setting and considered the Democratic Party's strong endorsement of group rights a sideshow or even a threat to their basic rights.

There is no doubt that the ugly head of immigration has now risen once again and could be the dominant issue in upcoming elections. The US has time and again frittered away golden opportunities to address this issue on a bipartisan basis. Even now, in 2024, the House and Senate are trying to cobble together a bipartisan bill that would address some of the major concerns, including the vast increase in immigrants across all categories. Other important issues, such as aid to Ukraine, are now being held hostage to the immigration question

My 14 ½ years at West Point and in the Army, culminating in my year in Vietnam, a war I opposed both before and after my service, have led me to conclude that we have made incredible mistakes in the national security arena over all the years of my adult life. This reached a crescendo with George Bush's graduation address at West Point in 2002, in which he announced his new approach to national defense, including his endorsement of "preventive war." When I read the speech, I called Senator Sarbanes, then a senior member of the Senate Foreign Relations Committee, and urged him to read it since it was a wholly new strategy which, if implemented, would place us not only as the guarantor of peace in many places of the world but also the principal nation aggressively seeking to prevent new conflicts anywhere. Bush was, of course, in that speech laying the groundwork for the subsequent invasion of Iraq in 2003.

I've enjoyed reading the books by Dr. Andrew Bacevich, Emeritus Professor of International Relations and History at Boston University. A West Point graduate, whose son, also a graduate, was killed in battle in Afghanistan, he received a PhD from Princeton and taught both at Hopkins and the academy before joining the Boston University faculty. His many books, such as "The Limits of Power," describe the course, starting with the Cold War, that led to our assuming the role of peacekeeper and arbiter in the affairs of the world. He points out the disastrous consequences of that role, including the shift of scarce national resources away from addressing the real problems of American society and the enormous loss of American lives in such places as Vietnam, Iraq, Syria, Afghanistan, Jordan, Somalia, Kenya and Lebanon. The astronomical cost of the endless and undeclared war on terrorism staggers the mind.

I've not read what he is now saying or writing about the Israeli/Palestinian/Houthis situation in the Middle East, but I can't imagine he is a proponent of further intervention. The US has, for years, ever since the founding of Israel in 1948, tried to play a lead role as the honest broker in the intractable conflict between the Palestinians and the Israelis efforts that have largely been ineffective. I believe such intervention, in light of the current

Israeli government and the leadership of Hamas, should be minimized.

There are multiple indicators of our slow slide into our present predicaments, including high rates of suicide, thousands of deaths from opioids, a decline in our life expectancy, the costliest health system in the world, and a nation with the highest percentage of obese citizens other than Samoa. Add to that an epidemic of loneliness, especially among our senior citizens. Robert Putnam's "Bowling Alone," when it was published, seemed somewhat alarmist; however, it clearly identified what had happened and what was happening in American society, isolating us from each other. The advent of social media has only served to expedite those changes.

I only wish we could continue to be emboldened by the hopes for our collective futures we once believed were such a solid element of the American experience. I particularly like this quote from one of my favorite historians, Eric Hobsbawm, since it speaks eloquently to those hopes: "...I understand 'barbarism' to mean two things. First, the disruption and breakdown of the systems of rules and moral behavior by which all societies regulate the relations among their members and, to a lesser extent, between their members and those of other societies. Second, I mean more specifically, the reversal of what we may call the project of the 18th century Enlightenment, namely the establishment of a universal system of such rules and standards of moral behavior, embodied in the institutions of states dedicated to the rational progress of humanity: to Life, Liberty, and the Pursuit of Happiness, to Equality, Liberty, and Fraternity...."

What has occurred in the last 35 years or so is the rise of fear as the driving force for our political environment. I love this quote from Tony Judt, one of my favorite political philosophers. "We have entered an age of fear. Insecurity is once again an active ingredient in Western democracies. Insecurity born of terrorism, of course, but also, and more insidiously, fear of the uncontrollable speed of change, fear of the loss of employment, fear of losing ground to others in an increasingly unequal distribution of resources, fear of losing control of the circumstances and routines of our daily life. And perhaps, above all, that it is not just **we** who can no longer shape our lives but that those in authority have also lost control to forces beyond their reach." Liberals and social democrats have played into these fears by concentrating public efforts on specific individuals and groups. However laudable those efforts have been, they have served to undercut the overarching view of government as a "general" practitioner of the art of governing in the interests of all the nation's people. President Trump has risen to power based solely on those fears and, in his second term, continues to rouse the public to increasingly irrational and inchoate fears.

And now the man of idyllic youth catalogues the woes we now face. I suppose in the face of the analysis I just conjured above; one would assume that I, in my semi-alert dotage, have given up. The United States has faced daunting challenges throughout its long history as the world's oldest democracy. Do I believe we have the capacity and the will to address these serious dilemmas once again? It is unlikely that I will know the answer to that question; however, I think the youngsters in America today have core beliefs and attitudes that could potentially lend themselves to solving these knotty problems. As the Germans say, "Gott Sei Dank."

Chapter 41

The End for Now

Not really the end. I am still thanking God each morning for allowing me to celebrate another day. I close with a poem I've loved for many years, ever since I first read it. I believe it is one of the greatest poems ever written. It is the work of a young, gay Englishman who hated war and yet volunteered to fight in World War One and was killed just days before the armistice. Harold Bloom opined that, had he lived, he would almost certainly have become one of the greatest 20th-century poets in the English language. He was Wilfred Owen -- now buried in a country churchyard but honored in poet's corner in Westminster Abbey as one of the great voices of that war.

In his poem, "Futility," Owen's sense of the tragedy of war and death is summed up in its opening lines regarding a dead soldier. It brings back haunting memories of those 13 dead Americans on a jungle hilltop in Vietnam.

"Move him into the sun -
Gently, its touch awoke him once,
At home, whispering of fields unsown.
Always it woke him, even in France,
Until this morning and this snow,
If anything might rouse him now
The kind old sun will know."

The poem I love is entitled "Strange Meeting." It is addressed to a German soldier and includes these simple but overwhelming lines: "Strange friend," I said, "here is no cause to mourn." "None," said the other, "save the undone years." This remarkable lament about war (as he calls it "the pity of war") ends with these lines: "I am the enemy you killed, my friend. I knew you in this dark; for so you frowned yesterday through me as you jabbed and killed. I parried, but my hands were loath and cold. Let us sleep now………" But my favorite part of the poem celebrates both his life and is, I posit, a premonition of his death.

"Whatever hope is yours, was my life also. I went hunting wild after the wildest beauty in the world, which lies not calm in eye or braided hair but mocks the steady running of the hour. And if it grieves, grieves richlier than here. For by my glee might many men have laughed, and of my weeping something had been left which must die now."

I have spent much of my life "hunting wild after the wildest beauty in the world." I shall continue to do so as long as God gives me breath and life.

"Qui vie sans folie n'est pas si sage qu'il quoit."

La Rochefoucault

Photos Enriching the Story

The tomb of St. Nicholas, Bari, Italy, where Father Kyrill and I sang the hymn to St. Nicholas while locked in his tomb

Father Mefodii and his happy Filipino students

Father Kyrill with Luba and Niko

Restored Pleasant Grove House & Summer
Kitchen, one of Marvin's proudest achievements

Marvin's design for the south façade of the
new Palmyra Fire station incorporating
John Hartwell Cocke's blind arches

Solar energy demonstration building
designed by Marvin

Epitaphian or Christ's Tomb Easter 2016

Master Iconographers of the Prosopon School Vladislav
Andreyev with the white beard in front row

Father Mefodii master Christmas tree decorator

Father Kyrill & his Cotswold garden hat

**Julann Griffin & Father Mefodii Marvin's 75th
Birthday Party Farmington Country Club -- 2012**

Judy's retirement party Glen Burnie

Marvin leading visitors on a tour of Glen Burnie's dining room

In 2010, I organized a West Point mini-reunion at Glen Burnie for 3 days with my company mates from Company K-1. Billy & Martha McDaniel are in the upper right corner. Unfortunately, most of the people in the photo have now reposed.

Marvin at his 60th West Point Reunion

Merry Monks

Judy and I receiving Preservation Piedmont's award for
restoration of the Pleasant Grove House

Acting Silly

England 2014 probably drinking wine
at Calke Abbey

Palladio's Villa Rotunda -- Vicenza

On the way to President Obama's inauguration January 2009
From left to right Joe Pegues' brother, Joe Pegues, Barbara van
Vooren, Nuha Abudabbeh, Marvin, Bettye Pegues
Steve the Dutchman, Theo van Vooren and Father Mefodii.

At my 2014 West Point reunion, the Army had just done away with
"Don't Ask; Don't Tell." I was curious about how it was working out
among the cadets and asked the authorities if I could meet with two
openly gay cadets. Here they are. We had a grand time. Both averred
that the academy was taking the change seriously. There is now a
gay club at West Point called "Knights Out." I love it.

West Point Founders Day 2024
The Oldest & the Youngest, Major Curtis Cranston
Class of 2012!